Principles and Standards for School Mathematics Navigations Series

NAVIGATING *through* DATA ANALYSIS *and* PROBABILITY *in* Prekindergarten–Grade 2

Linda Jensen Sheffield
Mary Cavanagh
Linda Dacey
Carol R. Findell
Carole E. Greenes
Marian Small

Carole E. Greenes
Prekindergarten–Grade 2 Editor
Peggy A. House
Navigations Series Editor

NATIONAL COUNCIL OF
TEACHERS OF MATHEMATICS

The National Council of Teachers of Mathematics, Inc.
1906 Association Drive, Reston, VA 20191-1502
(703) 620-9840; (800) 235-7566
www.nctm.org

ISBN 0-87353-520-0

Printed in the United States of America

Table of Contents

Contents of CD-ROM

About This Book

Navigating through Data Analysis and Probability in Prekindergarten–Grade 2 demonstrates how some fundamental ideas of data analysis and probability can be introduced, developed, and extended. The introduction to the book is an overview of the development of data and probability concepts from prekindergarten through grade 12, and the three chapters that follow it focus on important ideas of data and probability in prekindergarten through grade 2. Chapter 1 deals with data collection, organization, and display; chapter 2 suggests strategies for posing questions and displaying and analyzing data; and chapter 3 introduces simple probability.

Each chapter begins with a discussion of the foundational ideas and the expectations for students' accomplishment by the end of grade 2. This discussion is followed by student activities that introduce and promote familiarity with the essential ideas. At the beginning of each activity, the recommended grade levels are identified and a summary of the activity is presented. The goals to be achieved, the prerequisite knowledge, and the materials necessary for conducting the activities are specified. Some of the activities have blackline masters, which are signaled by an icon and identified in the materials list and can be found in the appendix. They can also be printed from the CD-ROM that accompanies the book. The CD, also signaled by an icon, contains applets for students to manipulate and resources for professional development.

All activities have the same format. Each consists of three sections: "Engage," "Explore," and "Extend." The "Engage" section presents tasks designed to capture students' interests. "Explore" presents the core investigation that all students should be able to do. "Extend" provides additional activities for students who demonstrate continued interest and want to do some challenging mathematics. Throughout the activities, questions are posed to stimulate students to think more deeply about the mathematical ideas. After some questions, possible responses are shown in parentheses. Margin notes include teaching tips, copies of blackline masters, and quotations from *Principles and Standards for School Mathematics* (National Council of Teachers of Mathematics 2000). The discussion section of each activity identifies connections with the process strands and other content strands in the curriculum, offers insights about students' performance, and suggests ways to modify the activities for students who are experiencing difficulty or who are in need of enrichment. Although grade levels are recommended, most of the activities can be modified for use by students at other levels in the pre-K–grade 2 band. In order to make the modifications that will most enhance students' learning, teachers are urged to observe students' performance by taking note of the appropriateness of their mathematical vocabulary, the clarity of their explanations, the robustness of the rationale for their solutions, and the complexity of their creations.

A cautionary note: This book is not intended to be a complete curriculum for data and probability in this grade band. It should, rather, be used in conjunction with other instructional materials.

Key to Icons

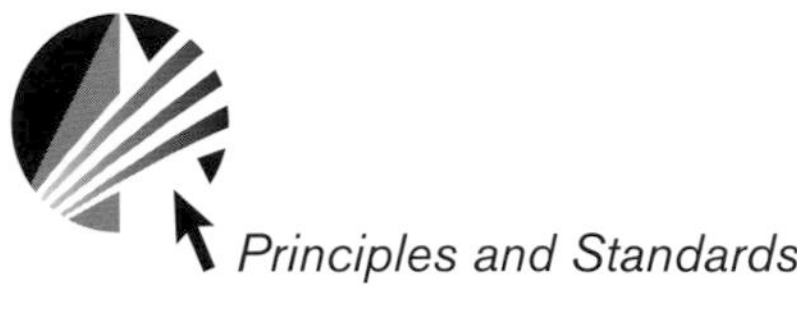

Principles and Standards

CD-ROM

Blackline Master

Three different icons appear in the book, as shown in the key. One alerts readers to material quoted from *Principles and Standards for School Mathematics,* another points them to supplementary materials on the CD-ROM that accompanies the book, and a third signals the blackline masters and indicates their locations in the appendix.

PRE-K–GRADE 2

DATA ANALYSIS *and* PROBABILITY

Introduction

The Data Analysis and Probability Standard in *Principles and Standards for School Mathematics* (NCTM 2000) is an affirmation of a fundamental goal of the mathematics curriculum: to develop critical thinking and sound judgment based on data. These skills are essential not only for a select few but for every informed citizen and consumer. Staggering amounts of information confront us in almost every aspect of contemporary life, and being able to ask good questions, use data wisely, evaluate claims that are based on data, and formulate defensible conclusions in the face of uncertainty have become basic skills in our information age.

In working with data, students encounter and apply ideas that connect directly with those in the other strands of the mathematics curriculum as well as with the mathematical ideas that they regularly meet in other school subjects and in daily life. They can see the relationship between the ideas involved in gathering and interpreting data and those addressed in the other Content Standards—Number and Operations, Algebra, Measurement, and Geometry—as well as in the Process Standards—Reasoning and Proof, Representation, Communication, Connections, and Problem Solving. In the Navigations series, the *Navigating through Data Analysis and Probability* books elaborate the vision of the Data Analysis and Probability Standard outlined in *Principles and Standards.* These books show teachers how to introduce important statistical and probabilistic concepts, how the concepts grow, what to expect students to be able to do and understand during and at the end of each grade band, and how to assess what they know. The books also introduce representative instructional activities that help translate the vision of *Principles and Standards* into classroom practice and student learning.

Fundamental Components of Statistical and Probabilistic Thinking

Principles and Standards sets the Data Analysis and Probability Standard in a developmental context. It envisions teachers as engaging students from a very young age in working directly with data, and it sees this work as continuing, deepening and growing in sophistication and complexity as the students move through school. The expectation is that all students, in an age-appropriate manner, will learn to—

- formulate questions that can be addressed with data and collect, organize, and display relevant data to answer them;
- select and use appropriate statistical methods to analyze data;
- develop and evaluate inferences and predictions that are based on data; and
- understand and apply basic concepts of probability.

Formulating questions that can be addressed with data and collecting, organizing, and displaying relevant data to answer them

No one who has spent any time at all with young children will doubt that they are full of questions. Teachers of young children have many opportunities to nurture their students' innate curiosity while demonstrating to them that they themselves can gather information to answer some of their questions.

At first, children are primarily interested in themselves and their immediate surroundings, and their questions center on such matters as "How many children in our class ride the school bus?" or "What are our favorite flavors of ice cream?" Initially, they may use physical objects to display the answers to their questions, such as a shoe taken from each student and placed appropriately on a graph labeled "The Kinds of Shoes Worn in Kindergarten." Later, they learn other methods of representation using pictures, index cards, sticky notes, or tallies. As children move through the primary grades, their interests expand outward to their surroundings, and their questions become more complex and sophisticated. As that happens, the amount of collectible data grows, and the task of keeping track of the data becomes more challenging. Students then begin to learn the importance of framing good questions and planning carefully how to gather and display their data, and they discover that organizing and ordering data will help uncover many of the answers that they seek. However, learning to refine their questions, planning effective ways to collect data, and deciding on the best ways to organize and display data are skills that children develop only through repeated experiences, frequent discussions, and skillful guidance from their teachers. By good fortune, the primary grades afford many opportunities—often in conjunction with lessons on counting, measurement, numbers, patterns, or other school subjects—for children to pose interesting questions and develop ways of collecting data that will help them formulate answers.

As students move into the upper elementary grades, they will continue to ask questions about themselves and their environment, but their questions will begin to extend to their school or the community or the world beyond. Sometimes, they will collect their own data; at other times, they will use existing data sets from a variety of sources. In either case, they should learn to exercise care in framing their questions and determining what data to collect and when and how to collect it. They should also learn to recognize differences among data-gathering techniques, including observation, measurement, experimentation, and surveying, and they should investigate how the form of the questions that they seek to answer helps determine what data-gathering approaches are appropriate. During these grades, students learn additional ways of representing data. Tables, line plots, bar graphs, and line graphs come into play, and students develop skill in reading, interpreting, and making various representations of data. By examining, comparing, and discussing many examples of data sets and their representations, students will gain important understanding of such matters as the difference between categorical and numerical data, the need to select appropriate scales for the axes of graphs, and the advantages of different data displays for highlighting different aspects of the same data.

During middle school, students move beyond asking and answering the questions about a single population that are common in the earlier years. Instead, they begin posing questions about relationships among several populations or samples or between two variables within a single population. In grades 6–8, students can ask questions that are more complex, such as "Which brand of laundry detergent is the best buy?" or "What effect does light [or water or a particular nutrient] have on the growth of a tomato plant?" They can design experiments that will allow them to collect data to answer their questions, learning in the process the importance of identifying relevant data, controlling variables, and choosing a sample when it is impossible to collect data on every case. In these middle school years, students learn additional ways of representing data, such as with histograms, box plots, or relative-frequency bar graphs, and they investigate how such displays can help them compare sets of data from two or more populations or samples.

By the time students reach high school, they should have had sufficient experience with gathering data to enable them to focus more precisely on such questions of design as whether survey questions are unambiguous, what strategies are optimal for drawing samples, and how randomization can reduce bias in studies. In grades 9–12, students should be expected to design and evaluate surveys, observational studies, and experiments of their own as well as to critique studies reported by others, determining if they are well designed and if the inferences drawn from them are defensible.

Selecting and using appropriate statistical methods to analyze data

Teachers of even very young children should help their students reflect on the displays that they make of the data that they have gathered. Students should always thoughtfully examine their representations to determine what information they convey. Teachers can prompt young children to derive information from data displays through questions like "Do more children in our class prefer vanilla ice cream, or do more prefer chocolate ice cream?" As children try to interpret their work, they come to realize that data must be ordered and organized to convey answers to their questions. They see how information derived from data, such as their ice cream preferences, can be useful—in deciding, for example, how much of particular flavors to buy for a class party. In the primary grades, children ordinarily gather data about whole groups—frequently their own class—but they are mainly interested in individual data entries, such as the marks that represent their own ice cream choices. Nevertheless, as children move through the years from prekindergarten to grade 2, they can be expected to begin questioning the appropriateness of statements that are based on data. For example, they may express doubts about such a statement as "Most second graders take ballet lessons" if they learn that only girls were asked if they go to dancing school. They should also begin to recognize that conclusions drawn about one population may not apply to another. They may discover, for instance, that bubble gum and licorice are popular ice cream flavors among their fellow first graders but suspect that this might not necessarily be the case among their parents.

In contrast with younger children, who focus on individual, often personal, aspects of data sets, students in grades 3–5 can and should be guided to see data sets as wholes, to describe whole sets, and to compare one set with another. Students learn to do this by examining different sets' characteristics—checking, for example, values for which data are concentrated or clustered, values for which there are no data, or values for which data are unusually large or small (*outliers*). Students in these grades should also describe the "shape" of a whole data set, observing how the data spread out to give the set its *range*, and finding that range's center. In grades 3–5, the center of interest is in fact very often a measure of a data set's center—the *median* or, in some cases, the *mode*. In the process of learning to focus on sets of data rather than on individual entries, students should start to develop an understanding of how to select *typical* or *average* (*mean*) values to represent the sets. In examining similarities and differences between two sets, they should explore what the means and the ranges tell about the data. By using standard terms in their discussions, students in grades 3–5 should be building a precise vocabulary for describing the characteristics of the data that they are studying.

By grade 5, students may begin to explore the concept of the mean as a balance point in an informal way, but a formal understanding of the mean and its use in describing data sets does not become important until grades 6–8. By this time, just being able to compute the mean is no longer enough. Students need ample opportunities to develop a fundamental conceptual understanding—for example, by comparing the usefulness and appropriateness of the mean, the median, and the mode as ways of describing data sets in different contexts. In middle school, students should also explore questions that are more probing, such as "What impact does the spread of a distribution have on the value of the mean [or the median]?" Or "What effect does changing one data value [or more than one] have on different measures of center—the mean, the median, and the mode?" Technology, including spreadsheet software, calculators, and graphing software, becomes an important tool in grades 6–8, enabling students to manipulate and control data while they investigate how changes in certain values affect the mean, the median, or the distribution of a set of data. Students in grades 6–8 should also study important characteristics of data sets, such as *symmetry*, *skewness*, and *interquartile range*, and should investigate different types of data displays to discover how a particular representation makes such characteristics more or less apparent.

As these students move on into grades 9–12, they should grow in their ability to construct an appropriate representation for a set of univariate data, describe its shape, and calculate summary statistics. In addition, high school students should study linear transformations of univariate data, investigating, for example, what happens if a constant is added to each data value or if each value is multiplied by a common factor. They should also learn to display and interpret bivariate data and recognize what representations are appropriate under particular conditions. In situations where one variable is categorical—for example, gender—and the other is numerical—a measurement of height, for instance—students might use appropriately paired box plots or histograms to compare the heights of males and females in a given group. By contrast, students who are presented with bivariate numerical data—for example, measurements of height and arm span—might use a scatterplot to represent their data, and they should be able to describe the shape of the scatterplot and use it to analyze the relationship between the two lengths measured—height and arm span. Types of analyses expected of high school students include finding functions that approximate or "fit" a scatterplot, discussing different ways to define "best fit," and comparing several functions to determine which is the best fit for a particular data set. Students should also develop an understanding of new concepts, including *regression*, *regression line*, *correlation*, and *correlation coefficient*. They should be able to explain what each means and should understand clearly that a correlation is not the same as a causal relationship. In grades 9–12, technology that allows users to plot, move, and compare possible regression lines can help students develop a conceptual understanding of residuals and regression lines and can enable them to compute the equation of their selected line of best fit.

Developing and evaluating inferences and predictions that are based on data

Observing, measuring, or surveying every individual in a population is an appropriate way of gathering data to answer selected questions. Such "census data" is all that we expect from very young children, and teachers in the primary grades should be content when their students confine their data gathering and interpretation to their own class or another small group. But as children mature, they begin to understand that a principal reason for gathering and analyzing data is to make inferences and predictions that apply beyond immediately available data sets. To do that requires sampling and other more advanced statistical techniques.

Teachers of young children lay a foundation for later work with inference and prediction when they ask their students whether they think that another group of students would get the same answers from data that they did. After discussing the results of a survey to determine their favorite books, for example, children in one first-grade class might conclude that their peers in the school's other first-grade class would get similar results but that the fourth graders' results might be quite different. The first graders could speculate about why this might be so.

As students move into grades 3–5, they should be expected to expand their ability to draw conclusions, make predictions, and develop arguments based on data. As they gain experience, they should begin to understand how the data that they collect in their own class or school might or might not be representative of a larger population of students. They can begin to compare data from different samples, such as several fifth-grade classes in their own school or other schools in their town or state. They can also begin to explore whether or not samples are representative of the population and identify factors that might affect representativeness. For example, they could consider a question like "Would a survey of children's favorite winter sports get similar results for samples drawn from Colorado, Hawaii, Texas, and Ontario?" Students in the upper grades should also discuss differences in what data from different samples show and factors that might account for the observed results, and they can start developing hypotheses and designing investigations to test their predictions.

It is in the middle grades, however, that students learn to address matters of greater complexity, such as the relationship between two variables in a given population or sample, or the relationships among several populations or samples. Two concepts that are emphasized in grades 6–8 are *linearity* and *proportionality*, both of which are important in developing students' ability to interpret and draw inferences from data. By using scatterplots to represent paired data from a sample—for example, the height and stride length of middle schoolers—students might observe whether the points of the scatterplot approximate a line, and if so, they can attempt to draw the line to fit the data. Using the slope of that line, students can make conjectures about a relationship between height and stride length. Furthermore, they might decide to compare a scatterplot for middle school boys with one for middle school girls to determine if a similar ratio applies for both groups. Or they might draw box plots or relative-frequency histograms to represent data on the heights of samples of middle school boys and high school boys to investigate the variability in height of boys of different ages. With the help of graphing technology, students can examine many data sets and learn to differentiate between linear and nonlinear relationships, as well as to recognize data sets that exhibit no relationship at all. Whenever possible, they should attempt to describe observed relationships mathematically and discuss whether the conjectures that they draw from the sample data might apply to a larger population. From such discussions, students can plan additional investigations to test their conjectures.

As students progress to and through grades 9–12, they can use their growing ability to represent data with regression lines and other mathematical models to make and test predictions. In doing so, they learn that inferences about a population depend on the nature of the samples, and concepts such as *randomness, sampling distribution*, and *margin of error* become important. Students will need firsthand experience with many different statistical examples to develop a deep understanding of the powerful ideas of inference and prediction. Often that experience will come through simulations that enable students to perform hands-on experiments while developing a more intuitive understanding of the relationship between characteristics of a sample and the corresponding characteristics of the population from which the sample was drawn. Equipped with the concepts learned through simulations, students can then apply their understanding by analyzing statistical inferences and critiquing reports of data gathered in various contexts, such as product testing, workplace monitoring, or political forecasting.

Understanding and applying basic concepts of probability

Probability is connected to all mathematics from number to geometry. It has an especially close connection to data collection and analysis. Although students are not developmentally ready to study probability in a formal way until much later in the curriculum, they should begin to lay the foundation for that study in the years from prekindergarten to grade 2. For children in these early years, this means informally considering ideas of likelihood and chance, often by thinking about such questions as "Will it be warm tomorrow?" and realizing that the answer may depend on particular conditions, such as where they live or what month it is. Young children also recognize that some things are sure to happen whereas others are impossible, and they begin to develop notions of *more likely* and *less likely* in various everyday contexts. In addition, most children have experience with common devices of chance used in games, such as spinners and dice. Through hands-on experience, they become aware that certain numbers are harder than others to get with two dice and that the pointer on some spinners lands on certain colors more often than on others.

In grades 3–5, students can begin to think about probability as a measurement of the likelihood of an event, and they can translate their earlier ideas of *certain, likely, unlikely*, or *impossible* into quantitative representations using 1, 0, and common fractions. They should also think about events that are neither certain nor impossible, such as getting a 6 on the next roll of a die. They should begin to understand that although they cannot know for certain what will happen in such a case, they can associate with the outcome a fraction that represents the frequency with which they could expect it to occur in many similar situations. They can also use data that they collect to estimate probability—for example, they can use the results of a survey of students' footwear to predict whether the next student to get off the school bus will be wearing brown shoes.

Students in grades 6–8 should have frequent opportunities to relate their growing understanding of proportionality to simple probabilistic situations from which they can develop notions of chance. As they refine their understanding of the chance, or likelihood, that a certain event will occur, they develop a corresponding sense of the likelihood that it will not occur, and from this awareness emerge notions of complementary events, mutually exclusive events, and the relationship between the probability of an event and the probability of its complement. Students should also investigate simple compound events and use tree diagrams, organized lists, or similar descriptive methods to determine probabilities in such situations. Developing students' understanding of important concepts of probability—not merely their ability to compute probabilities—should be the teacher's aim. Ample experience is important, both with hands-on experiments that generate empirical data and with computer simulations that produce large data samples. Students should then apply their understanding of probability and proportionality to make and test conjectures about various chance events, and they should use simulations to help them explore probabilistic situations.

Concepts of probability become increasingly sophisticated during grades 9–12 as students develop an understanding of such important ideas as *sample space*, *probability distribution*, *conditional probability*, *dependent* and *independent events*, and *expected value*. High school students should use simulations to construct probability distributions for sample spaces and apply their results to predict the likelihood of events. They should also learn to compute expected values and apply their knowledge to determine the fairness of a game. Teachers can reasonably expect students at this level to describe and use a sample space to answer questions about conditional probability. The solid understanding of basic ideas of probability that students should be developing in high school requires that teachers show them how probability relates to other topics in mathematics, such as counting techniques, the binomial theorem, and the relationships between functions and the area under their graphs.

Developing a Data Analysis and Probability Curriculum

Principles and Standards reminds us that a curriculum that fosters the development of statistical and probabilistic thinking must be coherent, focused, and well articulated—not merely a collection of lessons or activities devoted to diverse topics in data analysis and probability. Teachers should introduce rudimentary ideas of data and chance deliberately and purposefully in the early years, deepening and expanding their students' understanding of them through frequent experiences and applications as students progress through the curriculum. Students must be continually challenged to learn and apply increasingly sophisticated statistical and probabilistic thinking and to solve problems in a variety of school, home, and real-life settings.

The six *Navigating through Data Analysis and Probability* books make no attempt to present a complete, detailed data analysis and probability curriculum. However, taken together, these books illustrate how selected "big ideas" behind the Data Analysis and Probability Standard develop this strand of the mathematics curriculum from prekindergarten through grade 12. Many of the concepts about data analysis and probability that the books present are closely tied to topics in algebra, geometry, number, and measurement. As a result, the accompanying activities, which have been especially designed to put the Data Analysis and Probability Standard into practice in the classroom, can also reinforce and enhance students' understanding of mathematics in the other strands of the curriculum, and vice versa.

Because the methods and ideas of data analysis and probability are indispensable components of mathematical literacy in contemporary life, this strand of the curriculum is central to the vision of mathematics education set forth in *Principles and Standards for School Mathematics*. Accordingly, the *Navigating through Data Analysis and Probability* books are offered to educators as guides for setting successful courses for the implementation of this important Standard.

PRE-K–GRADE 2

DATA ANALYSIS *and* PROBABILITY

Chapter 1
Data Collection, Organization, and Display

Data can be thought of as information that is collected about people or objects, such as information for a United States Census or a health survey. Young children are naturally very curious about the world. Data collection helps them answer some questions that arise naturally as they try to understand the world that they see around them every day. For example, they might want to know what time other children have to go to bed each night, or they might be interested in finding out how many children like the food that is served in the cafeteria. Such interest gives teachers and parents opportunities to introduce the concepts underlying the study of statistics as early as preschool.

Statistics can be thought of as numerical descriptions of samples of the things that surround us. For children, these descriptions might be counts or measurements of people, favorite objects, or events that are important in their lives. *Statistics* also refers to the science or study of obtaining, organizing, and interpreting data to make decisions or to answer questions.

If children are to develop "data sense" very early, they first must be equipped with tools for gathering, sorting, and exhibiting data. "A fundamental idea in prekindergarten through grade 2 is that data can be organized or ordered and that this 'picture' of the data provides information about the phenomenon or question" (National Council of Teachers of Mathematics [NCTM] 2000, p. 49). Young children should experiment with organizing and displaying data in a wide variety of ways, and this work can lead to discussions about which methods of data organization and display are the most effective and the easiest to understand.

In this chapter, the activities focus on collecting, organizing, and displaying data. In Build a Graph, children use actual objects to make three-dimensional object bar graphs and then draw the corresponding two-dimensional bar graphs. Object bar graphs are also explored in All about Shoes, Chain It, Families, and What's Your Favorite? In Families, students also compare parts of the data set to the whole set when they compare data about brothers or sisters to the combined data about siblings.

A bar graph is a way to display information that uses bars of varying lengths to stand for the number of discrete pieces of data. Bar graphs are not used for continuous data, such as temperature or time. The bars may be either horizontal or vertical and may represent numerical data or other categories of data. For example, bars might show the members of a group of children in numerical categories (e.g., their ages, such as five, six, or seven years). Or the bars could represent the children in nonnumerical categories (e.g., the colors of their eyes, such as blue, brown, or green). The bars should be separate, not touching. In a vertical bar graph, the bars begin at the bottom, and in a horizontal bar graph, the bars begin at the left. All graphs should have a title. The bars make it easy for viewers to make visual comparisons of the sizes of groups.

Other methods for organizing and displaying data, including tallies and frequency tables, are explored in Chain It, Row Your Boat, and What's Your Favorite? The tally is one of the earliest methods humans used to keep track of quantities such as the number of sheep in a herd or the number of tools to be traded with another tribe of people. Young students learn that it is much easier to keep track of a tally if every fifth mark is a horizontal line segment that crosses the first four vertical ticks, as shown in figure 1.1. Many young students find that they are less likely to miscount if they use a horizontal mark—rather than a slanted one—across the other four ticks. Because students learn to count by fives at a very young age, they find that keeping track of objects using tallies helps them visualize the objects they are counting.

Fig. **1.1.**
A tally

A frequency table organizes data by using numbers to show how often an event happens. In the frequency table in figure 1.2, the number of students who voted for each dessert is shown.

Fig. **1.2.**
A frequency table

Favorite Dessert	Votes
Pie	6
Ice Cream	12
Cake	8

As students collect data, they should make tally marks, construct frequency tables from the tallied data, and then use the data in the tables to construct bar graphs. They will thus enhance their understanding of how these forms of data display are related. Teachers should also discuss with their students the differences and similarities among the various representations.

On the CD-ROM that accompanies this book, the applets for organizing data, Get Organized, and for making Venn diagrams, Shape Sorter, can give students practice with those skills.

In Junk Sort, students learn to use Venn diagrams to represent objects that they have sorted according to one or more attributes. A Venn diagram uses loops to show how objects are categorized and how they are related. For example, two nonintersecting loops may be used to show the number of boys and of girls in a classroom. Two intersecting loops may be used to show the number of girls in the class and the number of students in the class wearing shorts.

When students are first learning to sort and classify objects, they might begin by putting them in piles of objects that share a common attribute (e.g., all the objects are red or all are round) or a common function (e.g., all the objects are kitchen utensils or all are used to transport people). Young students may also classify objects together because they belong with each other (e.g., a student might put a male doll and a female doll in the same circle because they are "Mommy and Daddy and they belong together." At this beginning stage, students may not be consistent in their criteria for sorting. They might put the male doll and the female doll together because Mommy and Daddy belong together and then add a purse because Mommy needs her purse. Or they might put a blue triangle, a blue square, and a blue circle together and then add a red circle because it goes with the blue circle. Students may or may not be able to verbalize a rule for grouping the objects. Teachers may need to help the students verbalize their rules, and if the students are having difficulty, the teachers should ask questions to help the students clarify their thinking—for example, "This circle is for all the blue objects; is that blue?"

After students have some experience with sorting, they will be able to sort an entire collection of objects according to one rule. They could begin by sorting objects into two piles—those that belong and those that do not (e.g., all blocks that are red and all blocks that are not red). In such a simple task, a single attribute, for example, a color or a shape, is the sorting criterion. Students who are more advanced can sort objects into intersecting sets according to, for example, both color and shape. In such a task, students might put dogs in one category and black animals in another category and realize that black dogs must be placed in the intersection of the two loops representing the categories.

Students practice sorting objects and guessing rules for sorting while playing the game What's my rule? Students also learn to communicate their reasoning and justify it. The final activity in this chapter, Morley Most and Lutie Least, introduces students to picture graphs. Students collect data from and about their classmates and then use pictures to represent the collected data. Young students are curious about themselves and their immediate surroundings. This activity gives them an opportunity to explore their immediate world, to compare themselves with their classmates, to work cooperatively to solve a mathematical problem, and to practice their communication skills both verbally and graphically.

All the graphing activities afford students opportunities to analyze and talk about which methods give the clearest picture of the data collected. The choice of the best display to use depends on the information that is being represented and the way in which it will be used. The importance of labels on all types of data displays is emphasized in the activities.

Expectations for Students' Accomplishment

By the end of grade 2, students should be able to sort and classify objects according to two intersecting attributes, such as shape and color. Some students may have difficulty sorting objects into just two categories—objects that have a certain attribute and those that do not. With more experience, however, students should be able not only to categorize objects into distinct, nonintersecting categories but also to decide where objects belong in a Venn diagram if they possess none, one, or two of the specified attributes. Some students may be able to place objects in three intersecting categories, such as color, shape, and size, but such sophistication should not be expected until students complete grade 3.

By the end of grade 2, students should be able to construct and interpret object graphs, vertical and horizontal bar graphs, frequency tables, two-loop Venn diagrams, and tallies. In grades 3–5, those representations will be extended to include other such graphical forms as line graphs, three-loop Venn diagrams, and double-bar graphs.

By the end of grade 2, students should understand that titles and labels are needed on data representations so that the information can be interpreted correctly. The ideas about identification will be extended in grades 3–5.

Build a Graph

Prekindergarten–Kindergarten

Summary

Students sort cubes by color and construct three-dimensional, color-cube bar graphs. They use the graphs to compare the numbers of cubes of different colors and answer questions about the data displayed. They then construct two-dimensional bar graphs to show the same data.

Sort and classify objects according to their attributes and organize data about the objects

Goals

- Construct three-dimensional graphs
- Construct two-dimensional graphs to represent the data in three-dimensional graphs
- Interpret simple two- and three-dimensional graphs in horizontal and vertical forms

Prior Knowledge

- Counting up to ten objects
- Identifying the numerals 0 through 10
- Identifying colors
- Identifying some bars as taller, longer, or shorter than others
- Comparing two sets of objects to determine which has more (or fewer) objects or if both sets have the same number of objects

Materials

- Forty colored linking cubes, ten of each of four colors
- Four containers—one for each color—to hold the cubes
- Four three-inch-by-five-inch index cards, each colored to match a different color of cube and with the name of the color printed on the card
- One copy of the blackline masters "Vertical Graph Mat" and "Horizontal Graph Mat" for each student. If you are using cubes that are two centimeters on an edge, copy the blackline masters at 133 percent; if the cubes are one inch on an edge, copy them at 167 percent.
- Crayons
- A poster-board graph having squares the same size as the faces of the cubes and labeled with the numerals 0–10, as shown in figure 1.3
- Removable cellophane tape
- Velcro

pp. 80, 81

Activity

Engage

Seat the students in a circle. Place the forty colored cubes on the floor. Hold up four cubes, one of each color, and call on students to identify the colors. Then have a pair of children sort all the cubes by color. Ask other students to count the cubes of a particular color and tell the number. Have the students then place all the cubes of each color in a separate container.

Explore

Call on each of four students to take one handful of cubes of the same color, with each student selecting a different color. Have each of those students count the cubes and tell the number of cubes of her or his color. Show the students the color cards. Point to and read the names of the colors. Arrange the cards in a row on the floor or a table.

Call on students to place or connect the cubes of each of the four colors face-to-face to make cube "trains." Position the trains vertically above the corresponding color cards (see fig. 1.4). Talk about the arrangement of the cube trains. Say, "This is a bar graph. It is called a *bar graph* because each of the trains (*point to the colored-cube trains*) looks like a bar. The bar graph makes it easier for us to compare the numbers of cubes of different colors."

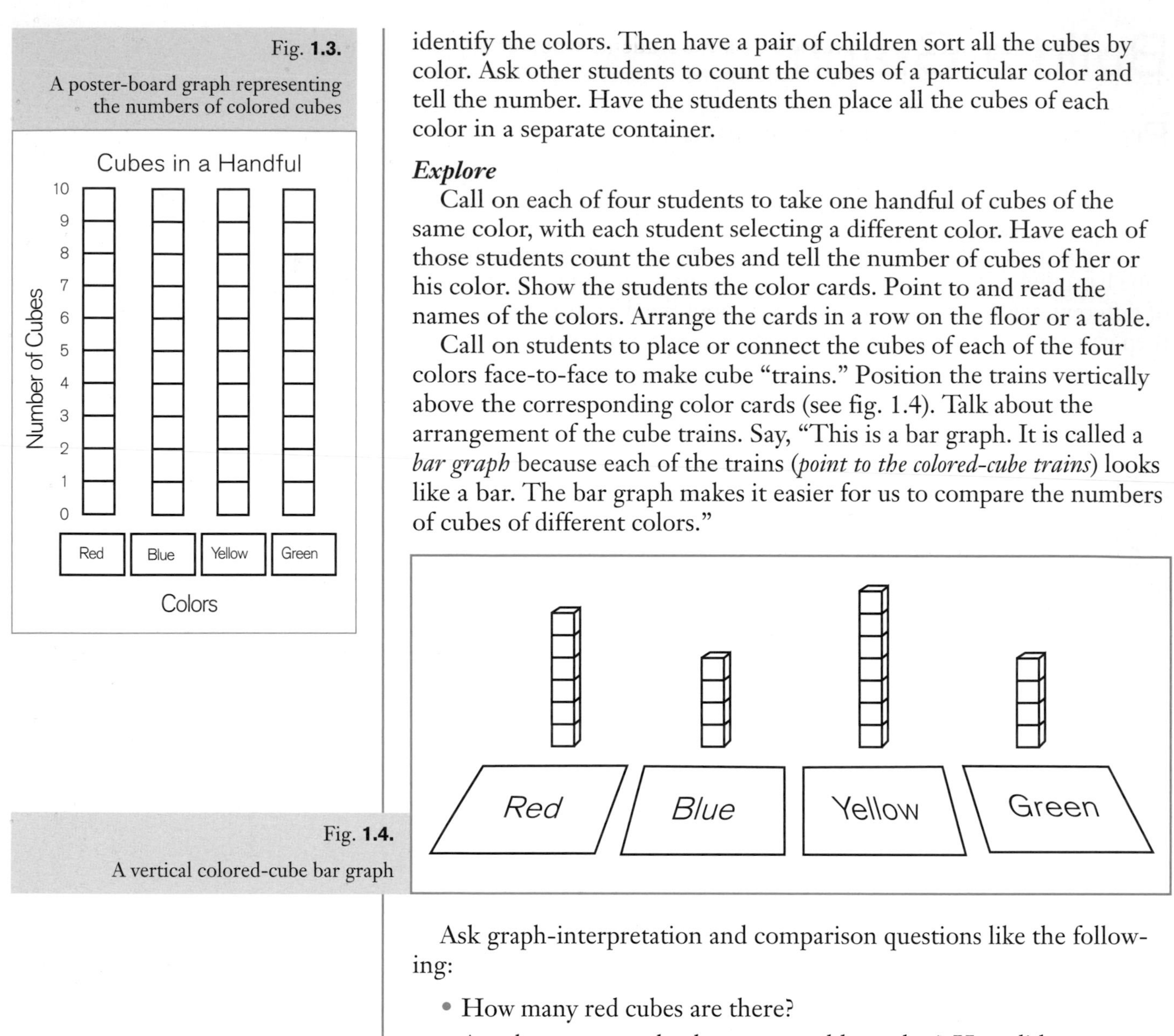

Fig. **1.3.**
A poster-board graph representing the numbers of colored cubes

Fig. **1.4.**
A vertical colored-cube bar graph

Ask graph-interpretation and comparison questions like the following:

- How many red cubes are there?
- Are there more red cubes or more blue cubes? How did you decide? If the students give counting as their method of comparison, ask, "Can you tell without counting? Yes, you can compare the bars. The red bar is taller than the blue bar. So there are more red cubes than blue cubes."
- Are there fewer blue cubes or yellow cubes? How did you decide? If both sets contain the same number of cubes, ask, "What can you say about the numbers of blue cubes and yellow cubes? (They are the same.) How can you tell from the graph? (The bars are the same height.)

Repeat this activity with other groups of four children. Have the students build the bars from the bottom up. Be sure that the cubes in each bar are stacked neatly face-to-face.

Tell the students that the bar graph can also be made in a different way. Use one of the last vertical graphs made by a group of students. Arrange the color cards above one another on a table or other flat surface, turn the cube trains so that they are horizontal (i.e., arranged left to right), and place the trains to the right of the color cards (see fig.

1.5). Ask the same questions as before. Ask the students whether any of the answers to the previous questions changed when the orientation of the bars changed from vertical to horizontal. Point out to the students that the tallest bar has become the longest one.

Extend

Set up the poster-board graph shown in figure 1.3, and tape color cards in the rectangles along the bottom of the graph. Call on students to identify the numbers on the graph. Have four students arrange their handfuls of cubes on the poster-board graph (attach strips of Velcro to the cubes and to the squares on the poster board), and call on students to identify the number of each color. Demonstrate how to read across a graph, from the top of a bar to the number on the left of the graph. Have the students count the cubes to verify that their reading of the number on the graph is correct. Ask questions that elicit comparisons of the information represented by the bars, as before. Include questions that require the students not only to make comparisons but also to tell "how many more" and "how many fewer."

Give each student a copy of the blackline master "Graph Mat." Have the children make two-dimensional representations of their group's three-dimensional vertical graph. As you walk around the room, question the students about their graphs.

Discussion

Build a Graph not only introduces students to the construction and interpretation of bar graphs but also gives them practice in counting and in comparing sets of objects—two big ideas in the number strand. As students count to tell how many more or fewer, you will be able to note if they are counting systematically and if they understand the comparison terms *more* and *fewer*.

Having students compare the vertical and horizontal graphs also reinforces relationships involved in measurement. Students see that the tallest bar becomes the longest bar when the bar graph is rotated. They also observe that to compare the bars, the bars must have a common beginning point or baseline. For more practice with this activity, you may wish to have the students use the graphing applet, Get Organized, on the CD-ROM that accompanies this book.

Fig. **1.5.**
A horizontal colored-cube bar graph

You may want to have the students make two-dimensional copies of horizontal colored-cube bar graphs. If so, distribute copies of "Horizontal Graph Mat" for the students to complete.

What's Your Favorite?

Prekindergarten–Kindergarten

Summary

Students participate in surveys of their classmates to collect information about each person's favorite pet, color, or fruit. Using photographs or drawings of themselves that are all the same size, they construct and interpret bar graphs of their "favorites."

Pose questions and gather data about [students] and their surroundings

Represent data using concrete objects, pictures, and graphs

Goals

- Construct and conduct minisurveys
- Use tally marks to represent objects or colors
- Organize data in tables
- Organize data in bar graphs
- Interpret tables and bar graphs

Prior Knowledge

- Counting up to twenty objects
- Identifying the numerals 0 through 20
- Comparing the numbers of objects in sets to tell which has more (or fewer) or the most (or the fewest)
- Identifying bars in a graph that are the tallest (or taller), the longest (or longer), and the shortest (or shorter)

Materials

- A poster-board graph that has three-inch squares to hold the photographs or drawings of the students and that has been labeled with the numerals 0–20 (See the example of a poster-board graph in fig. 1.3.)
- Unlined, white, three-inch-by-five-inch index cards, one for each choice (pet, color, fruit) in the class's surveys, to use as labels for bar graphs
- Twenty unlined index cards of each of four different colors
- One pencil for each student
- Three large pieces of poster board for graphs
- A photograph or drawing of each student, mounted on three-inch-square cards (which can be cut from index cards)
- Removable cellophane tape
- A black marking pen

Activity

Engage

Show the students the unlined index cards in the four different colors, with the appropriate color names written on them. Print the names of the colors on the board. Ask, "Can you tell from looking at this list which of these four colors most students like best? What could we do to find out?"

Use removable cellophane tape to attach the cards to the bottom of the poster-board graph. Distribute the mounted photographs or drawings to the students. Tell them that they will be making a bar graph to show their favorite color. Say, "First you have to decide which of these four colors is your favorite. You can choose only one. When I say the name of your favorite color, raise your hand. Then come to the graph and put your picture above the name of the color." Name each color in turn. Help the students attach their photos neatly to the graph, beginning at the bottom. When all the photos have been attached, ask questions like the following:

- What are the numbers along the side of the graph? (0 through 20)
- How many students picked red as their favorite color? How do you know? (We counted; we read the number from the graph.)
- Which color is the class's favorite? How can you tell from the graph? (The bar above it has the most photos; it has the tallest bar.)
- Which color is the class's least favorite? How can you tell from the graph? (The bar above it has the fewest photos; it has the shortest bar.)
- How many more people picked red than yellow?
- How many fewer people picked blue than green?

Explore

Remind the students that one purpose of collecting data is to answer a particular question. Conduct a minisurvey that can be used to answer a question about favorite pets. First have the students identify animals that can be house pets. Then call on a student to choose four of the animals to use in the survey. Have the students help you select a title and make the labels for another poster-board graph. Record the names of the animals on index cards. If pictures (stickers or small drawings) of the animals are available, attach them to the cards to aid in reading the animals' names. Call on a student to attach the labels to the bottom of the poster-board graph so that the data can be represented in a meaningful way.

"The main purpose of collecting data is to answer questions when the answers are not immediately obvious." (NCTM 2000, p. 109)

Appoint a student to conduct the survey by naming each pet in turn. Have the students arrange their photos in columns above the label for their favorite pets. Ask the same kinds of graph-interpretation questions that you asked for the graph of favorite colors. You might have the students make a horizontal bar graph as well as a vertical bar graph to represent this information.

Extend

Choose another question that the students are interested in answering, such as what their favorite fruits are so that they can help the school cafeteria decide which fruit to offer for lunch. Have the students identify four different fruits that might be offered, and ask the children to suggest a way to represent the favorite-fruits data so they can share the information with the cafeteria manager. One way is to record the names of the fruits in a column on the board. Label the column "Fruit." Call on the students, one by one, to choose a favorite fruit from the list. As each child names a fruit, make a tally mark next to that fruit, and label the column “Tally of Fruits.” When five students have named a fruit, demonstrate how to make the fifth tally mark by drawing a horizontal mark across the four vertical marks. After all the students have responded, label a third column “Number of Fruits,” and call on a student to count the tally marks and record the number to the right of the tallies to complete the table (see fig. 1.6).

Fig. **1.6.**
A table of favorite fruits

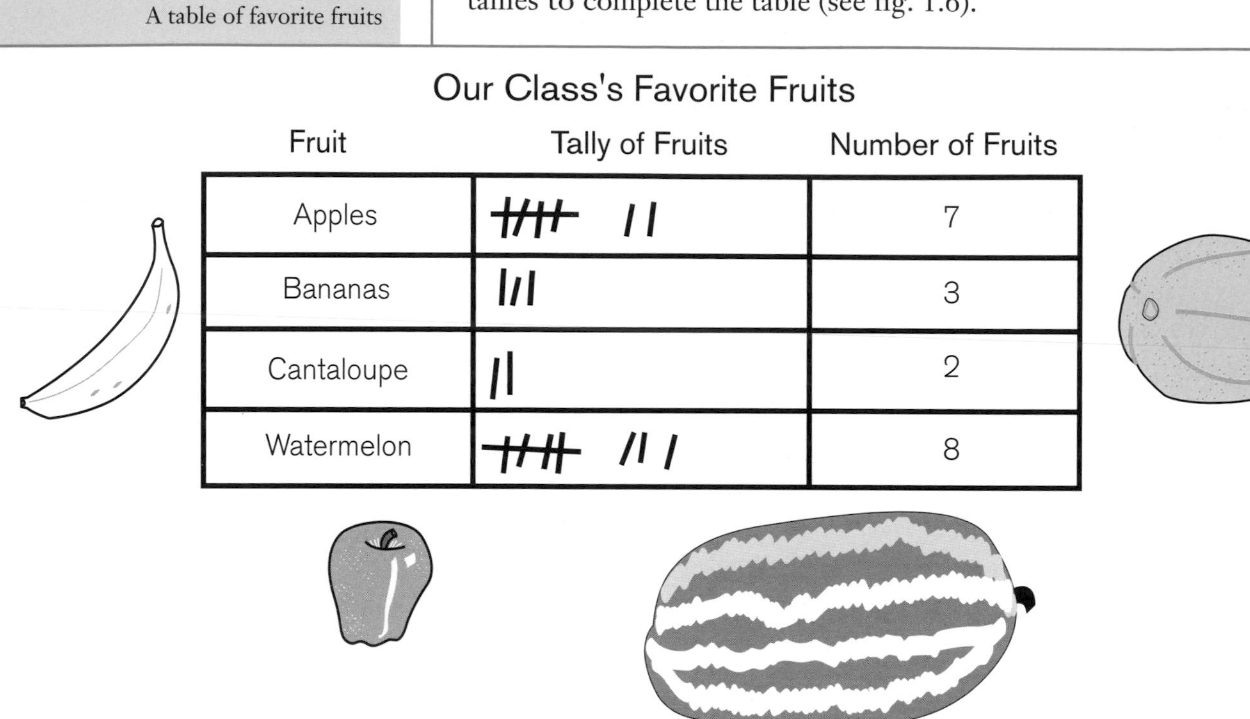
Our Class's Favorite Fruits

Fruit	Tally of Fruits	Number of Fruits
Apples	𝍸 ||	7
Bananas	|||	3
Cantaloupe	||	2
Watermelon	𝍸 |||	8

Ask the same types of interpretation and comparison questions about the table that you asked about the bar graphs. Show the students how to use the numbers in the table to construct a bar graph. From index cards, make a label for each fruit. Have the students construct the bars with blank index cards of different colors, with one color representing each kind of fruit. Talk about how the table and the bar graph are alike and how they are different. (They both show the kinds of fruit and the number of each kind selected. In the table, a tally mark represents a selected fruit, whereas in the bar graph, a card stands for a selected fruit. In the table, the total number of each kind of fruit selected is given, whereas in the bar graph, the number of each kind selected must be determined by looking from the top of the bar to the number label on the graph or by counting the number of cards in each bar.) Ask, “To identify the class’s favorite fruit, which is easier to use—the table or the bar graph? Why do you think so?”

As a follow-up, the students can conduct surveys to discover favorite vegetables, ball games, stories, or songs.

Discussion

What’s Your Favorite? not only develops students’ understanding of different ways to organize and represent data but also provides practice in skills from other strands. When students organize data in tables and bar graphs and interpret the displayed information, they gain experience with the number skills of counting, recording numerals, and comparing numbers of elements in two or more sets. As they compare the heights of the bars in the bar graph to determine which item is the favorite, they apply skills learned in the measurement strand.

In addition to having the class use the data-organization schemes in this activity, allow the students to develop their own methods of data organization. After the students have collected data, you might ask them to suggest a method of organization or you might show them how another class organized its data and ask your students to compare the two methods.

Junk Sort

Prekindergarten–Grade 2

Summary

Students discuss how materials found in the classroom are alike and different and then sort the materials using attributes suggested by the teacher or by other students. They then play the game What's my rule? and identify the secret rule or rules that the teacher or other students used to sort the materials. Venn diagrams are used as a means of representing relationships between sets of objects.

Sort and classify objects according to their attributes and organize data about the objects

Goals

- Recognize, compare, and sort objects on the basis of various attributes
- Use Venn diagrams to sort and classify objects and to display data

Prior Knowledge

- Identifying attributes of everyday objects
- Understanding the meaning of *alike* and *different*
- Identifying the attributes by which sets of objects have been sorted

Materials

- A variety of classroom objects to sort (e.g., pens, pencils, crayons, blocks, paint jars, attribute blocks)
- Yarn or other materials (e.g., plastic hoops) for making loops for Venn diagrams
- A large paper bag

Activity

Engage

Collect an assortment of classroom materials, such as pens, pencils, crayons, blocks, and small toys, and place them in a bag. Seat the students in a circle so that they can all see you, the bag, and one another. Take two objects—for example, a red pen and a yellow pencil—out of the bag, and ask, "How are these alike?" Encourage a variety of responses, such as "You can write with both of them," "They are both about the same length as my hand," or "They are both long and skinny." After the students have given several responses, ask them to tell you how the pen and the pencil are different.

"Young students begin by using their own vocabulary to describe objects, talking about how they are alike and how they are different."
(NCTM 2000, p. 97)

Take another object, such as a yellow block, out of the bag. Ask what is alike about the block and either the pen or the pencil. Again, encourage a variety of responses, such as "The block and the pencil are the same color" or "They both fit in my hand." Then ask the students to tell you some things that are different about the block and the pencil.

Have the students take turns removing objects from the bag and giving a variety of ways the new object is like or different from one or more of the objects that were previously removed from the bag.

Choose one of the likenesses suggested by the students, such as "They are both yellow," and sort all the objects into two piles—those that have that attribute and those that do not.

Explore

Engage students in the game What's my rule? To begin, choose a rule that describes two or more objects that are in the bag, but do not announce the rule. For example, you might choose the rule "I can write with it." Have the students take turns removing objects from the bag and asking whether the objects fit your rule. Then answer yes or no, and direct the students to put the objects in one of two piles—one for objects that fit your rule and one for those that do not fit your rule. When several objects are in both piles, encourage the children to guess your rule. The first child to guess the rule wins and becomes the rule maker for the next game. Have the student whisper the rule to you before beginning the round so that you can be prepared if the student forgets the rule or does not respond correctly to his or her classmates.

"Organizing data into categories should begin with informal sorting experiences ... [that] help develop an understanding of 'things that go together,' while building a vocabulary for describing attributes and for classifying according to criteria."
(NCTM 2000, p. 109)

Extend

Students who are adept at sorting objects into two piles might try playing the game with two different rules. For example, you might have one rule that the object is yellow and a second rule that the object is something the students can write with. To model this game with Venn diagrams, begin with nonoverlapping loops, as shown in figure 1.7. When first playing this game, tell the students that the loop on the left is for yellow objects and the loop on the right is for objects that they can write with. Give the children objects from the bag such as a yellow block and a red crayon and direct them to place the objects in the correct loops. Be sure to include objects that do not fit either rule, such as a red block, and have the children place such objects in a pile outside both loops.

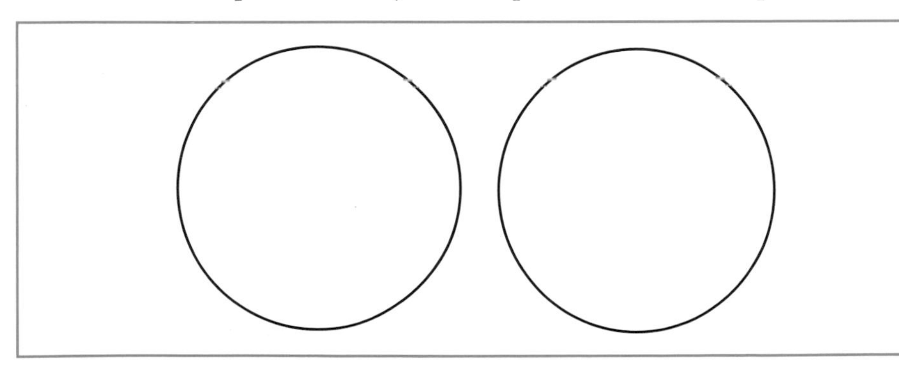

Fig. **1.7.**
Nonintersecting loops for a Venn-diagram model of What's my rule?

Show the students a yellow pencil or a yellow crayon, and ask them to decide where to place the objects. Encourage the students to talk about why the objects belong in both loops. Lead them to the realization that the loops can be overlapped, as shown in figure 1.8, and put the objects in the intersection of the loops.

Students who are successful with this activity can continue to play other two-rule games in which two students decide on the rules for the two loops and the other students decide where to place the objects.

The applet Shape Sorter, on the CD-ROM, includes activities that give students more experience in using Venn diagrams to classify materials.

Discussion

Preschool children may be quite familiar with describing what is alike and what is different about objects from watching television shows

Fig. **1.8.**

Intersecting loops for a Venn-diagram model of What's my rule?

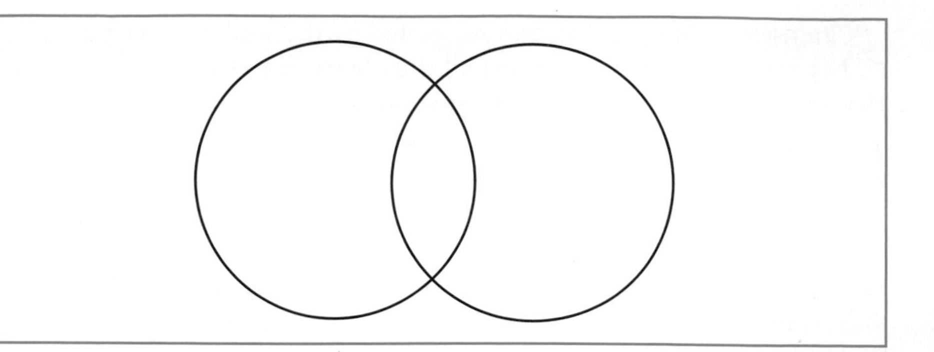

like *Sesame Street* or from playing games that emphasize these concepts. This type of activity helps students understand the concepts of *similarity* and *difference* and affords opportunities to use the vocabulary appropriate to those concepts. The game What's my rule? encourages children to analyze the attributes of objects to determine whether the objects have the characteristic that fits the secret rule.

Some preschool children and many kindergarten children will be ready to move to sorting objects using two attributes simultaneously. Some may even be able to play a more complex version of What's my rule? in which they identify two rules for intersecting sets (e.g., the objects are red and round). Young children are likely to need adult supervision to ensure that the objects are placed correctly according to both the attributes.

If commercial attribute materials such as attribute blocks, People Pieces, or Connecting People are available, you might want to use those materials for some of the games of What's my rule?

As students move from sorting materials to organizing data, they may not automatically transfer skills from the one type of activity to the other. In the next activity, All about Shoes, students sort their shoes and then organize the data about the shoes into object bar graphs.

All about Shoes

Kindergarten

Summary

Each student contributes one shoe to form a collection of shoes. Students sort their shoes by such attributes as color, type of closure (Velcro, shoestrings) or absence of closure, type of sole (hard or rubber), right or left foot, and type of shoe (sneaker or other types). Using actual shoes, students construct "real" (object) bar graphs on the floor.

Goals

- Sort objects by their attributes
- Describe the properties used to sort a group of objects
- Organize data in a systematic way
- Compare sets of objects to tell which has more (or the most) or fewer (or the fewest)

Prior Knowledge

- Identifying similarities and differences
- Counting up to twenty-five objects

Materials

- One shoe from each child
- One-half-inch-wide masking tape
- A floor graph with two columns (Use masking tape on the floor or on butcher paper. Make each square about eight inches by eight inches.)

Activity

Engage

Begin by telling the students that a local shoe store would like to know what types of shoes kindergarten students wear. Explain that this information will help the store decide what shoes to order. Have the students brainstorm questions that the shoe store might be interested in, such as What colors do you wear? What type of closure do you like? What are the soles of your shoes like?

Ask the students how you might use their shoes to collect some data to share with the shoe store. One way is to have each student contribute one shoe to a group of shoes on the floor. (Each student should put a slip of paper with his or her name in the shoe before adding the shoe to the pile.) Be sure that all the students can see the shoes. Pick up one of the shoes. Call on a student to describe the shoe. He or she might say, for example, "It is a blue sneaker," or "It has a rubber sole and shoestrings." Select one of those attributes—say, shoestrings—and call on students to identify other shoes that have that attribute. Repeat the process for shoes that have other attributes—for example, hard soles, Velcro

Ten cells in each column of your floor graph will probably be adequate. When shoes no longer fit on the graph, the children will see how to continue the graph. Have them help you extend the graph to accommodate the additional shoes.

closures, buckles, two colors, bumpy (or smooth) soles, a "tongue," or right (or left) fit.

Explore

Select one of the attributes of shoes, such as rubber soles. Have the students separate all the shoes that have that property from those that do not. Place the shoes with the attribute in one column on the floor graph and shoes without the attribute in the other column. Label the first column as the selected property and the second column as *not* that property. Ask questions like the following about the graph:

- Which column has more shoes?
- Which column has fewer shoes?
- Are there more shoes with rubber soles or with soles that are not rubber? How many more (fewer)? How do you know?
- How many students have shoes on the graph?

Extend

Use a three- or four-column graph and an attribute of shoes such as color. Have the students sort their shoes by the attribute and then construct an object bar graph with the shoes on the floor. Talk about the likelihood that another class would have the same number of shoes displayed on a bar graph for the same attribute. Say, for example, "If Mrs. DiMillo's class made a graph of the colors of their shoes, do you think most of their shoes would be blue?"

"They should discuss when conclusions about data from one population might or might not apply to data from another population."
(NCTM 2000, p. 109)

Discussion

This sorting-and-graphing activity uses a personal item of interest to children, their shoes. Using real objects enhances their interest in the activity and sets the stage for developing their understanding of ways to organize information.

The everyday activities of classifying objects, sorting objects into groups, analyzing and interpreting classifications, and drawing conclusions are some of the essential intellectual tasks that people perform. These lifetime skills begin well before kindergarten. Graphing is an extension of students' natural interest in sorting objects. It is a powerful tool that young children can use to arrange information and establish order.

Chain It

Grades K–1

Summary

Working in groups of three, students are given a specified amount of time to make "the longest chain possible." The number of links in each chain is then displayed in a bar graph.

Goals

- Make predictions about quantity and length
- Conduct an experiment
- Make tally marks to represent objects
- Display data in more than one way
- Construct and interpret bar graphs

Prior Knowledge

- Counting to fifty

Materials

- Rectangular strips of paper about one inch by eight inches
- Cellophane tape or glue sticks for each group of students
- Paper and pencils for each group of students
- Three-inch-square sticky notes
- A paper chain with twenty links

Activity

Engage

Show the students a paper chain with twenty links. Ask, "How do you think this chain was made?" After several students have shared their ideas, let them select a technique for constructing their own chains. Allow time for each student to make a three-link chain using the agreed-on technique.

Using their short chains as an aid, have the students estimate the number of links in the long chain. Then, as you point to each link in the long chain, have the students count the links aloud. Say, "Suppose that you made a chain like this by yourself. Then suppose you made another one like this in cooperation with other students. Which would take more time—the chain you made alone or the one you made by working together?"

Explore

Have the students, working in groups of three, predict the number of links in the chain they think they can make in one minute. (The time may be increased depending on the dexterity and counting abilities of your students.) Ask each group to record their prediction on a sheet of paper. Distribute tape or glue sticks, a sheet of paper for recording, and

rectangular strips to each group. Explain that as each link is added to the chain, one member of the group should make a tally mark on the piece of paper. Allow time for the groups to decide how they will complete the task.

Give the signal to start, and allow the groups to work until the designated time has passed. At the signal to stop, have the groups verify that the number of tally marks is the same as the number of links in their chains. Say, "How could we show the total number of links in every group's chain?" The students may make a variety of suggestions, such as raising their hands for different numbers, making tallies on the board, or writing their numbers on sticky notes and placing them on a chart. Follow a couple of the students' suggestions so that they can see more than one display of their data. Have the students compare the actual data with their predictions.

Ask the following questions:

- Which group made a chain with the fewest links? How many links are in its chain?
- Which group made a chain with the most links? How many links are in its chain?
- What numbers of links are between these two numbers? (Name the least number of links and the greatest number of links, and record the numbers between them.)

Write all those numbers, spaced about four inches apart, in order near the bottom of the board. Have all the students in each group write their names on a single sticky note and place the group's note above the number corresponding to the number of links in the group's chain. Be sure that all the students can see the bar graph, and ask them to describe the data.

Students tend readily to note the greatest and the least number of links. You can encourage them to make other observations as well by asking questions such as these:

- How many groups made chains with more than eight links?
- Tell us something about our data using the words *many more*, *three fewer*, and *twice as many as*.
- If a new group of students joined us, how many links do you think they could make in one minute? Why do you think so?

Extend

After the students have discussed their data, ask them if they think the data would change if—

- they repeated the activity;
- the second-grade students made the chains;
- they were allowed to work for two minutes;
- they worked in larger or smaller groups.

Change one of the variables (e.g., the number in the group, the amount of time), and have the students repeat the experiment. Then ask the students to compare the two data sets. If this activity is done early in the school year, you may want to save these data and repeat the experiment toward the end of the year.

"One rule is important about collecting and compiling data: never throw anything out. The information collected by your students can be used again to compare data sets and see change over time." *(See Basile [1999, p. 11], on the CD-ROM.)*

Discussion

By organizing their data in bar graphs, students can better recognize patterns and variation. Graphical displays allow young children to detect gaps in the data and to see how much the data are spread out, where the data are clustered, and which values are most common. Exposing students to bar graphs, a standard form of representation, adds to the techniques from which they can later choose to represent new data.

Once data are organized, it is important that students analyze and interpret the data rather than just respond to such factual questions about them as "How many groups made chains with nine links?" At this level, the emphasis should be on comparing parts of the data set (e.g., "More groups made eight links than made ten links") and on describing the shape of the data (e.g., "Most chains had between twelve and fourteen links"). Questions about how the data would change if the conditions of the experiment were altered provide opportunities for students to interpret the situation and compare their existing data sets so that they can make well-considered predictions.

"As students work with numerical data, they should begin to sort out the meaning of the different numbers—those that represent values ('I have four people in my family') and those that represent how often a value occurs in a data set (frequency) ('Nine children have four people in their families')." (NCTM 2000, p. 109)

Families

Grades 1–2

Summary

Students collect and display data to show the numbers of sisters and of brothers they have. They then combine these data sets to create a display of the number of siblings they have.

Goals

- Collect, organize, and display data
- Describe and analyze data
- Combine data to answer a new question

Prior Knowledge

- Experience in collecting and representing data
- Counting or adding to find sums

Materials

- Class lists
- Materials for displaying data (e.g., paper, sticky notes, linking cubes, chain links, crayons)
- *A Very Special Sister*, by Dorothy Hoffman Levi (1992) (or another book about brothers and sisters)

Activity

Engage

Gather the children, and read them a story about brothers and sisters. One book they may find interesting is *A Very Special Sister*, by Dorothy Hoffman Levi (1992). This book tells the story of Laura, a young deaf child. Laura is excited about becoming a big sister. She is worried, however, that because her new sibling might be able to hear, she or he might be more loved by their mother.

Explore

Ask the students to predict the number of sisters most of their classmates have. To help them make their predictions, you might ask, "Do you think anyone has fifteen sisters?" To avoid later confusion, ask, "Can you be your own sister?" After this initial conversation, tell the students that they will find out how many sisters each student has.

Show the children the materials they might use to collect and record data. The materials could include blank paper, graph paper, sticky notes, linking cubes, chain links, or crayons. Let the children decide individually how best to collect the data, and give them ample time to do so. Have class lists available so that the students can use them to keep track of the students who have been surveyed. When the students have completed this part of the task, ask, "What did you learn from your data?" Encourage a variety of responses. Next say, "I have a friend who wants to know how many sisters each of us has. I'd like you to make a display of our data that you think my friend would find helpful." Again, let the children decide how best to record the information they have collected.

Once the displays have been completed, encourage the students to present them. Ask questions such as the following:

- What does this display show?
- Which display best shows the number of sisters most of us have?
- Which display best shows how many sisters each of us has?
- Which display do you think is easiest to read?

These questions are not intended to imply that one display is best. Rather, they help the students realize that different displays have different advantages. Encourage the students to justify their choices by explaining why they chose a particular display.

On the following day, ask the students to repeat the processes of data collection and data display, focusing this time on the number of brothers. When this task has been completed, ask if anyone knows the meaning of the word *sibling*. Once the students understand the word, ask them to discuss how they could figure out the number of siblings their classmates have. If no student suggests combining the two sets of data they have already collected, prod them by asking, "Could our data help us answer this question?" The students can then apply their counting and addition skills to determine the number of siblings. Individual students can display those data as they think best.

Extend

To reinforce the idea that sometimes previously collected data can answer new questions, ask the students to identify other questions they could answer if they knew—

- the number of houses on the west side of a street that runs north-south and the number of houses on the east side of that street;
- the number of students in the class and the number of boys in the class;
- the number of students in the school who bought lunch on Monday and the number of students in the school who bought lunch on Tuesday (be sure to discuss why this information might not be used to determine who bought lunch on both days).

Discussion

Too often, teachers decide how data will be displayed. Although such an approach allows data to be organized quickly, it does not permit students to wrestle with the decision themselves. Although time consuming, the process of deciding how best to organize and display data is an important experience for students.

When students are encouraged to create their own representations, their work is often quite varied. They may attend to different aspects of the data or choose to display the same data in different ways. In one second-grade class, Kyra made a stick figure for each student in the class. She then drew on each figure a number sign (much like those worn in a race) that showed the number of sisters for that student. Brad

"Through constructing their own representations, students become more familiar with their data, with numerical relationships, and with the connection between the action of counting, the objects that they count, and the symbols that represent these quantities."
(Russell and Stone 1990, p. 52)

found the total number of brothers, twenty-seven, and drew that number of boys surrounding a large "27." Galena grouped her data and showed the number of students who had no sisters, one sister, and so on. Such diversity of work intrigues students and supports robust mathematical discussions in the classroom.

Row Your Boat

Grades 1–2

Summary

Students examine the frequency of words and letters in various familiar songs and use tally marks and frequency tables to record and display their collected data.

Pose questions and gather data about themselves and their surroundings

Goals

- Pose questions and gather data to answer the questions
- Represent and describe data using tally marks
- Display data by constructing frequency tables

Represent data using concrete objects, pictures, and graphs

Prior Knowledge

- Identifying the first, the second, and the third of three events that occur over time
- Counting to twenty

Create and use representations to organize, record, and communicate mathematical ideas

Materials

- Chart paper with the words to "Row, Row, Row Your Boat" and, below the words, a separate vertical listing of each word that occurs in the song (The illustration in fig. 1.9 shows such a list in which the occurrences of the words have been tallied.)
- Chart paper with the words to "Mary Had a Little Lamb" and a separate vertical list of the words
- Colored markers
- A copy of the blackline master "Mary Had a Little Lamb" for each student (optional)

p. 82

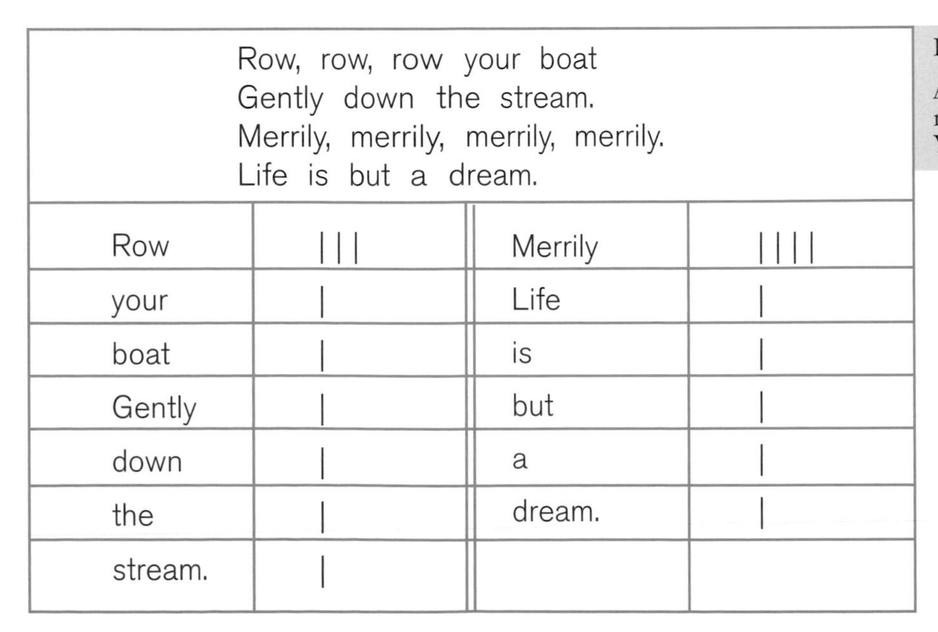

Row, row, row your boat
Gently down the stream.
Merrily, merrily, merrily, merrily.
Life is but a dream.

Row	|||	Merrily	||||
your	|	Life	|
boat	|	is	|
Gently	|	but	|
down	|	a	|
the	|	dream.	|
stream.	|		

Fig. **1.9.**

A chart showing the tally of the occurrences of each word in "Row, Row, Row Your Boat"

Activity

Engage

With the students, sing the song "Row, Row, Row Your Boat." As you sing, point to the words on the chart paper. Ask the students why they think that words are often repeated in songs. (It emphasizes the words and makes them easier to remember.)

Call on a student to name a word that appears in the lyrics more than once. Point to the word on the chart paper. With the students' help, circle all occurrences of the word using one colored marker. If both the words *row* and *merrily* are identified, use two colored markers, one for *row* and one for *merrily*. Discuss the positions of the words as they are mentioned (e.g., *boat* is the fifth word; *row* is the first, second, and third word.)

Point to the list of words below the song. Read the words one at a time with the students. Call on students to count the number of times each word appears in the song. Make the appropriate number of tally marks to show the number of occurrences (see fig. 1.9). Convert the tally chart into a frequency table (see fig. 1.10).

Fig. **1.10.**

A frequency table for the words in "Row, Row, Row Your Boat"

Occurrences of the Words in "Row, Row, Row Your Boat"

Word	Frequency
Row	3
your	1
boat	1
Gently	1
down	1
the	1
stream	1
Merrily	4
Life	1
is	1
but	1
a	1
dream	1

Ask questions such as these:

- Do most words occur more than once or just once?
- Which word occurs most often?
- In which positions in the song is that word?
- Why is it hard to identify the word that occurs least often?

Explore

Show the chart paper on which you have written the lyrics to "Mary Had a Little Lamb." Have the students record all the different words in the song (or hand out to each student a copy of the blackline master "Mary Had a Little Lamb"). Have the students circle each word in the rhyme, using the same color for all the occurrences of a word, and create a tally chart and a frequency table to show the number of times each word appears in the song. (Jeremy's work is shown in fig. 1.11. In spite of having carefully used color coding, Jeremy has some omissions in his chart.) Talk with the students about whether there is more repetition in this song than in "Row, Row, Row Your Boat," and ask them to explain their answers.

Ask the students how they can use the tally chart (or the frequency table) to tell—

- how many words are actually in the song;
- how many different words are in the song;
- which word occurs most often;
- which words occur more than once;
- where the most-repeated words are positioned in the song.

Extend

The students could create tally charts and frequency tables using a different song with repetitive lyrics (perhaps one that is particularly popular in the class), or they could make a tally chart or frequency table for the letters that appear in a line of one of the songs they have already explored. (See the example in figure 1.12.) Alternatively, if the students are familiar with musical notation, you could show them music for one of the songs already explored and ask them to create a tally chart and frequency table showing the repetition of notes.

Fig. **1.11.**

One student's tally chart and frequency table for "Mary Had a Little Lamb"

Jeremy

Mary had a little lamb,
little lamb, little lamb.
Mary had a little lamb.
Its fleece was white as snow.

	Tally Marks	Frequency
Mary	||	2
had	||	2
a	||	2
little	||||	4
lamb	||||	4
Its	|	1
fleece	|	1
was	|	1
white	|	1
as		1
snow	|	

Occurrences of Letters in the First Line of "Mary Had a Little Lamb"

M	||
A	||||
R	|
Y	|
H	|
D	|
L	|||
I	|
T	||
E	|
B	|

Occurrences of Letters in the First Line of "Mary Had a Little Lamb"

Letter	Frequency
M	2
A	4
R	1
Y	1
H	1
D	1
L	3
I	1
T	2
E	1
B	1

Fig. **1.12.**

A tally chart and a frequency table for the letters in the first line of "Mary Had a Little Lamb"

Discussion

It is important that students collect and analyze data about information of interest to them. Songs have universal appeal, and songs with a lot of repetition are particularly appealing.

One of the most important things to observe is how the students go about collecting their data (i.e., how they ensure that they have not overlooked any information and how carefully they tally their data). Some students may prefer going directly to the frequency table, finding the tally chart an unnecessary step. But making the tally marks first is the optimal way for other students to organize their data.

Morley Most and Lutie Least

Grade 2

Summary

The focus of this activity is on the construction and interpretation of graphs. Students are presented with several picture graphs to which they add the data for their class. They then learn to title, label, and interpret the graphs. They also examine displays of additional data and determine which characteristics of the data appear most and least often.

Goals

Describe parts of the data and the set of data as a whole to determine what the data show

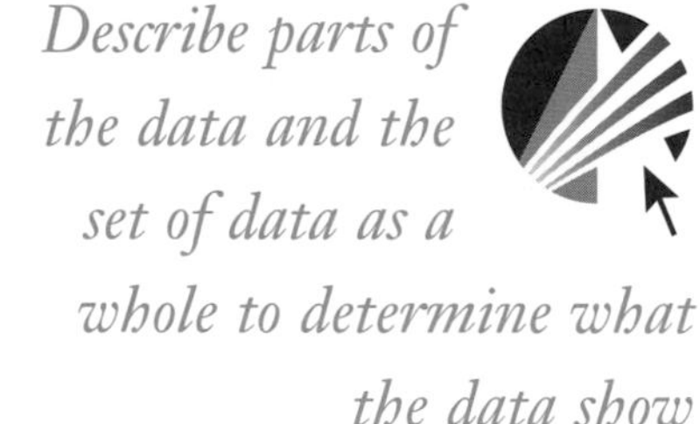

- Interpret bar and picture graphs
- Represent data using bar and picture graphs
- Describe parts of the data displayed in bar and picture graphs
- Decide on the basis of the data displayed in bar and picture graphs which event is most or least likely

Prior Knowledge

- Computing sums to twenty
- Computing differences between numbers that are less than twenty

Materials

- Medium-sized (about 3″ by 3″) sticky notes
- Grid paper with one-inch or two-centimeter squares (available on the CD-ROM)
- Six sheets of newsprint, large graph paper, or poster board on which to construct graphs
- Markers
- Pencils and paper
- Crayons
- One copy of each of the following graphs: "Ages of Students," "Number of Students' Pets," "Number of Students' Siblings," "Students' Favorite Sport." All the graphs are available on the CD-ROM. These graphs could be enlarged for ease of viewing. They should be adapted to reflect the number of students in your class.

Activity

Engage

Before beginning this activity, use newsprint, large grid paper, or poster board to make a graph like the one shown in figure 1.13. Attach the graph to a bulletin board or wall so that the students can easily reach it. Give each student one sticky note. Say, "Draw a palm-up picture of the hand or hands you use to write, and write 'right,' 'left,' or

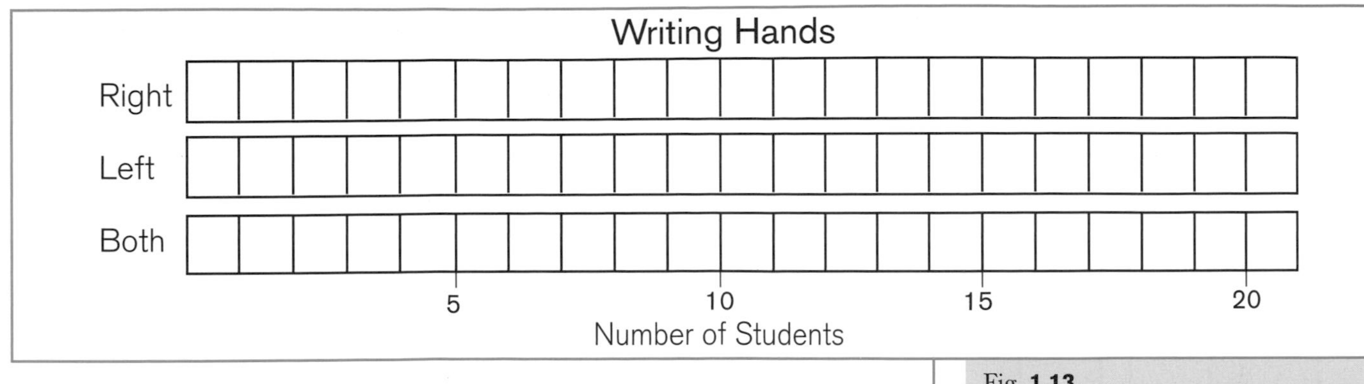

Fig. **1.13.**

A hand-preference graph prepared with a title, labels, and rows of squares

'both' on this square." When the students have finished with their drawings, show them the graph. Call on students to read the title and the labels on the graph. Have them stick their drawings on the graph in the appropriate spots. Discuss the importance of placing the drawings carefully next to each other and of beginning on the left with the square next to the label "Right," "Left," or "Both." When the graph has been completed, it should look similar to the one in figure 1.14.

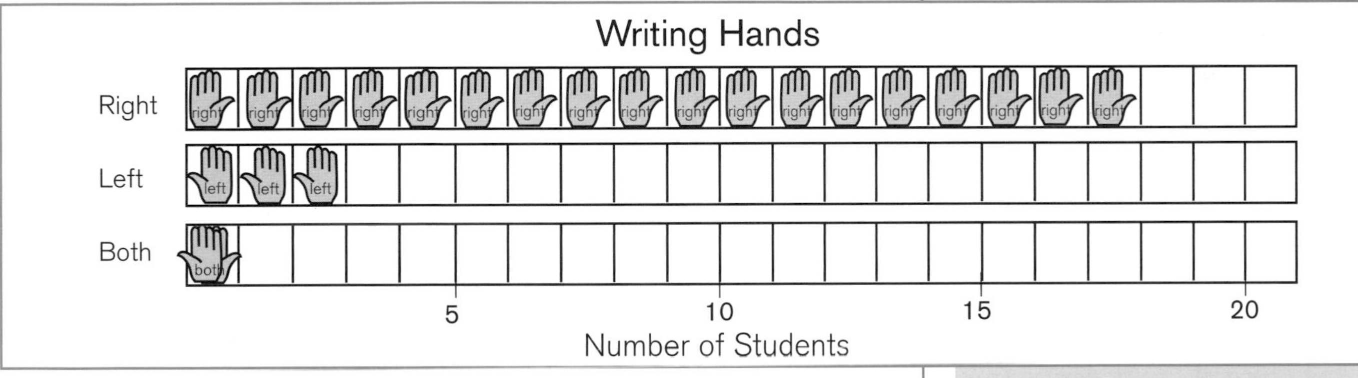

Fig. **1.14.**

A completed hand-preference graph

Make the boxes on the graph the same size as the sticky notes to outline a consistent area for the children's pictures, which will help ensure that the graph is accurate.

Ask questions like the following:

- What is the title of the graph? ("Writing Hands")
- Why is the title important? (It tells us what the graph shows.)
- What are the categories? (right, left, both)
- Do more people write with their left hand or with their right hand? (with their right hand)
- How many more people write with their left hand than with both hands? (Two more write with their left hand in the graph shown. The answers for other classes will vary.)
- How many people can write with either hand? (One can write with both hands in the graph shown. The answers for other classes will vary.)
- Suppose that one person in your class is chosen to write on the board. Which hand do you think the student will use to write? Explain your choice. (The student will most likely use the right hand because more people use their right hand than their left hand.)

Explore

Give the students another sticky note on which to draw and color pictures of their eyes. When they have finished, tell them that you want

Fig. **1.15.**

Columns prepared for a graph of the color of students' eyes

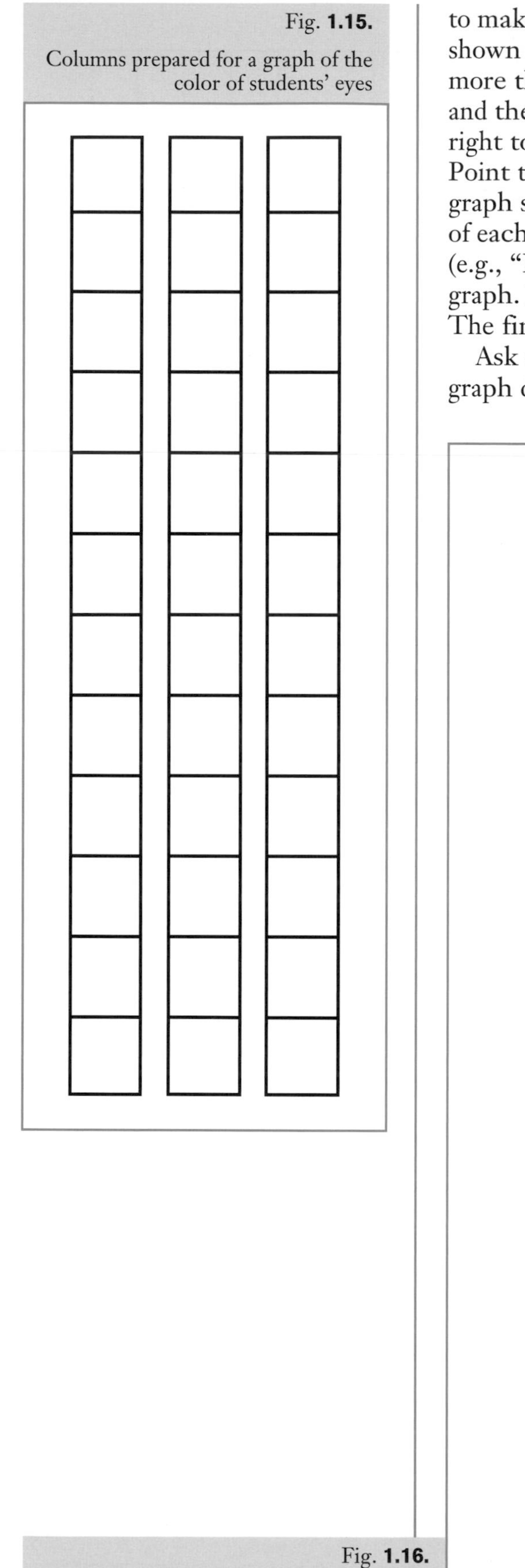

to make a graph for eye color. Display columns of squares like those shown in figure 1.15 (add columns as necessary if the students report more than three colors). Talk about the differences between this graph and the writing-hands graph. (The writing-hands graph goes left to right to make rows. This graph goes bottom to top to make columns.) Point to the title on the writing-hands graph, and ask what this new graph should be titled. (Eye Color) Point to the labels at the beginning of each row on the writing-hands graph. Ask the students what labels (e.g., "Brown," "Blue," and "Green") you should write on the eye-color graph. Have the students put their sticky notes in the appropriate spots. The finished graph should look similar to the one in figure 1.16.

Ask questions like the following. (The answers are based on the graph displayed in fig. 1.16. The answers for other classes will vary.)

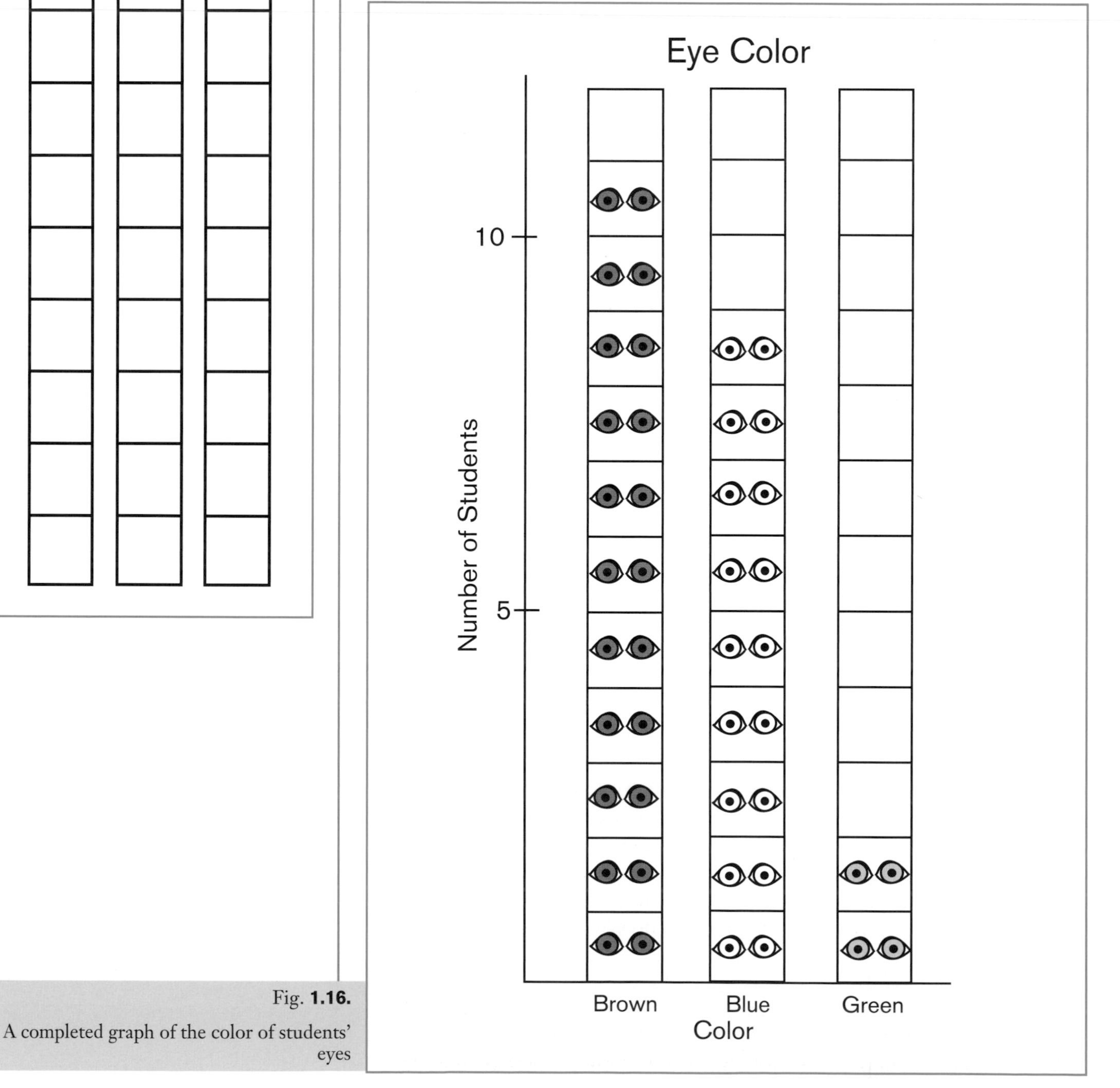

Fig. **1.16.**

A completed graph of the color of students' eyes

- What is the title of the graph? (Eye Color)
- What are the categories? (brown, blue, green)
- Do more people have brown eyes or blue eyes? (brown eyes)
- How many more people have brown eyes than blue eyes? (two more)
- Do more people have brown eyes or eyes that are not brown? (The same number have brown eyes as have eyes that are not brown.)
- Suppose that one person in your class is chosen in secret. What color do you think the student's eyes will be? Explain your choice. (brown because more students have brown eyes)

Extend

Adapt the copies of the four graphs "Ages of Students," "Number of Students' Pets," "Number of Students' Siblings," and "Students' Favorite Sport" to reflect the number of students in your class. These graphs are shown in figure 1.17 and are also available on the CD-ROM. You may want to enlarge the additional graphs, tape them to cardboard, and stand them on the chalk tray. Ask questions to help the students understand each graph, and discuss the characteristics that occur the most often and least often in each graph. When the class has completed its discussion, have each student write a story about Morley Most and Lutie Least. Tell them that Morley Most has the most-common characteristics shown in the graphs and Lutie Least has the least-common ones. Have the students illustrate the stories with pictures of Morley and Lutie showing these characteristics. Be sure that the characteristics the students give in their stories agree with the data in the graphs. With the given data, for instance, a child might write the following:

> Morley Most is 7. He has brown eyes and writes with his right hand. He has one brother but no sisters and has only one pet. He likes baseball.
>
> Lutie Least has green eyes and is 6 years old. She uses her left hand to write. She has four pets. She has four brothers and sisters. Hockey is her favorite sport.

You might also read the students a statement and ask them if it could possibly be true, given the data on the graphs. Say, for example, "All the seven-year-olds like soccer best." Since the graphs show that there are more seven-year-olds than there are students who like soccer best, the students should be able to tell you that your statement could not be true.

Discussion

The construction and the interpretation of graphs are important concepts in contemporary mathematics curricula. It is important that students be able to identify the parts of a graph, describe the categories, and compare the numbers of students in each category. Young students tend to remember things about themselves better than things about other people; thus they are more likely to understand and relate to the data about themselves. The ideas presented in this activity are fairly sophisticated, but if assigned categories and a prepared graph are used, the difficulty level is appropriate for this grade band. One of the most common errors in students' graphs is that the amount of space allocated to the data points is not consistent. This error is avoided by

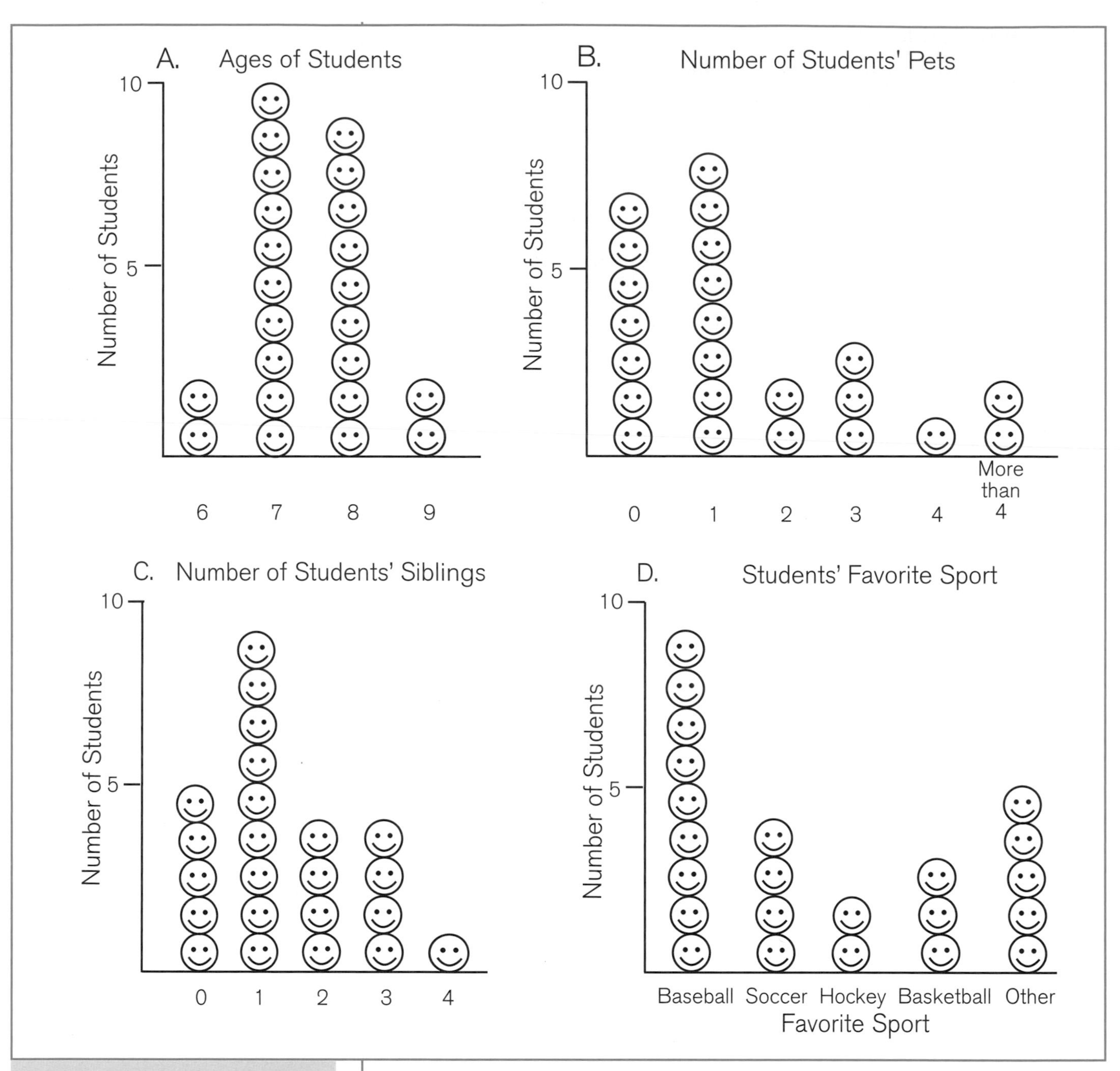

Fig. **1.17.**

Four graphs students can use to write stories about Morley Most and Lutie Least

using pictures drawn on squares of the same size and by using squares for data entry.

As the students discuss their graphs, be sure that each child can identify the most common and least common characteristic for each graph. If the stories they write for the last task do not reflect the data for the class, individual interviews will help you find their misconceptions. For example, a child might write about her favorite eye color, not the most common eye color according to the class data.

Conclusion

The first chapter has focused on gathering, sorting, and exhibiting data. The second chapter builds on these skills to lead children to pose questions and analyze data.

PRE-K–GRADE 2

DATA ANALYSIS *and* PROBABILITY

Chapter 2
Question Posing and Data Analysis

The explorations in this chapter focus on helping students learn to pose and critique questions whose answers are of interest to them. Building on their natural curiosity and desire to find out more about their world, students then collect data to answer the questions and learn to analyze and interpret the data. Alan Graham (1987) outlined four components that are typically seen in a statistical investigation. He refers to them as the "PCAI model." Although originally applied to explorations conducted by secondary school students, the four stages are equally appropriate for investigations conducted by preschool through second-grade students. The four steps follow:

- *Pose the question.* At this stage, students decide on specific questions of interest and determine the data that are needed to arrive at answers.
- *Collect the data.* Students decide on the best way to collect the data and then collect it. This step builds on the skills described and developed in chapter 1 of this book.
- *Analyze the data.* Analysis includes organizing, summarizing, describing, and displaying the data, as discussed and developed in chapter 1, but it carries the process further. Students also look for patterns and variations among the data.
- *Interpret the results.* At this stage, students use the results of their analysis of the data to answer their original questions.

The skill of posing a question is central to the activity Conducting a Survey, in which students learn to collect data to answer questions when the answers are not obvious. As children work on developing surveys, they will probably realize that most problems are not well defined. They may have to rewrite their survey questions several times before the questions are specific enough to elicit the answers that interest them.

The activities in chapter 1 are designed to help students learn techniques for organizing and displaying data. In this chapter, the investigations help students learn that data can be collected in a variety of ways. In these explorations, students will gain experience in conducting surveys and counting and measuring to quantify data. In the activities in chapter 3, students will conduct simple experiments to gather data.

In describing the data that they collect, students will begin to use a few simple terms to describe measures of central tendency (ways of reporting data in the middle of a range) and measures of dispersion (ways of reporting how spread out the data are). These terms include the following:

- *Mean*—the arithmetic average, the number found by adding all the relevant values and dividing by the number of addends
- *Median*—the value found by ordering the values of interest from the highest to the lowest and identifying the value in the middle if there is an odd number of values or averaging the two middle values if there is an even number
- *Mode*—the most frequently occurring value in a data set
- *Range*—the difference between the highest value and the lowest value

Initially, students will use simple techniques for analyzing the data that they collect and data that are displayed in graphs that they encounter in their everyday lives. In the activity Back and Forth, students learn to translate data they have collected and represented in one type of graph to another type of graph. Mystery Graphs and Whom Do You Believe? require students to analyze information presented in different forms; these activities lead them to discuss ways in which data might be misleading. In Travel Agent, students learn to use the data they have collected to make informed decisions. In What a Difference a Day Makes, students begin to see how graphs can help them visualize changes.

One of the goals of the activities in this chapter is for students to begin to realize the importance of data collection in making informed decisions. They should notice that answering a question often requires more than just giving an opinion. Analyzing facts and data is important to making good choices. Some questions will not have clear-cut answers, but students should begin to use data to support their conclusions, even if different children reach different conclusions on the basis of the same information. Using real data collected by the students is often the best way to help them realize that they can raise questions and make informed decisions if they carefully construct questions, collect and analyze data, and interpret the results.

Expectations for Students' Accomplishment

By the end of grade 2, students should have begun to refine the questions they use as the basis of their surveys and have had experience using a variety of methods for keeping track of the responses to their questions. They should be able to analyze the data collected in order to answer their questions and support their conclusions. They should have begun to question inappropriate methods of data collection and inappropriate statements about results. They should have some basic understanding that consistency in scale is also important in order to avoid misrepresentations of data. Making predictions on the basis of data involves informal discussions at this level. More-formal methods of interpreting data will be used in grades 3–5.

In prekindergarten through grade 2, students informally discuss simple inferences and predictions based on data that they collect, but these ideas will not be developed in any depth until the next grade band. Further development requires an understanding of sampling, which will be explored in grades 3–5. At this level, however, students' discussions of sampling will be limited to simple ideas, such as whether other groups might get the same results or reach the same conclusions if they took a similar survey. For example, students who have surveyed the bedtimes of the children in their first-grade class might discuss whether the results would be the same for seventh-grade students or for parents.

The applet Get Organized, included on the CD-ROM, offers students a variety of ways to develop their graphing capabilities further.

Back and Forth

Grades K–1

"As students' questions become more sophisticated and their data sets larger, their use of traditional representations should increase.... They should be using counts, tallies, tables, bar graphs, and line plots." *(NCTM 2000, p. 109)*

Summary

Students collect data about such topics as their favorite method of preparing potatoes or their favorite pizza toppings. They display their data and explore and compare different forms of display, such as tables, tally charts, picture graphs, or horizontal or vertical bar graphs.

Goals

- Display data in more than one way
- Collect and represent data using tables, tallies, picture graphs, and bar graphs

Prior Knowledge

- Counting to twenty

Materials

- A raw, unpeeled potato in a paper bag or box
- Three-inch-by-three-inch squares of paper or sticky notes
- Large blank sheets of butcher or chart paper
- Three-inch-by-five-inch index cards
- Crayons
- Double-sided cellophane tape
- Readily available materials that can be used to create graphs, such as colored squares of paper, chart paper with three-inch-by-three-inch grids, linking cubes, blocks, tiles, clothes pins, and roping or ribbon

Activity

Engage

Hide a potato in a paper bag or a box, and identify it as the "mystery bag" or "mystery box." Tell the students that they should try to guess what is in the bag or box by asking you yes-or-no questions about its attributes (e.g., "Is it red?" "Is it round?" "Can we eat it?"). Many children will have difficulty asking such questions at first. They may be inclined to ask what the item is (e.g., "Is it a teddy bear?" "Is it a cookie?"). You may need to give them examples of appropriate questions about color, size, shape, function, where they might find it, and so on. After they have asked several questions, you might have them tell you what they have learned about the item. List the information on the board, and then continue with the questioning.

Once the students have guessed that the mystery item is a potato, ask them how potatoes can be prepared. List their ideas (baked, french fried, mashed, fried into chips or hash browns, etc.) on the board.

Explore

Narrow the list to three or four favorite ways to have potatoes. Ask the children to draw a picture of their favorite way on three-inch-by-three-inch-square pieces of paper or sticky notes. Have the students initial their drawings and randomly tape or stick them to a large sheet of chart or butcher paper. You may want to draw a large outline of a potato on the paper, as shown in figure 2.1. Discuss the data displayed. Ask, "What can we tell about your favorite ways to have potatoes prepared? What type of cooked potato does most of the class prefer? How many more prefer fries than prefer chips?"

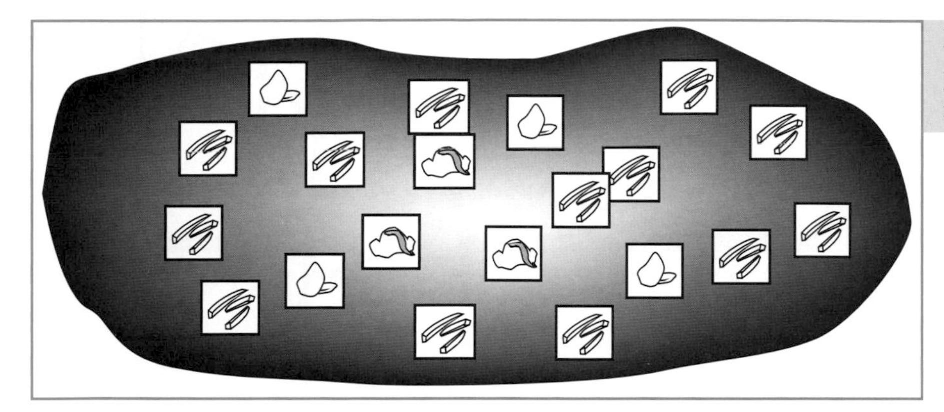

Fig. **2.1.**

Randomly placed drawings of students' favorite kinds of cooked potatoes

Discuss the usefulness of the display with the children. Ask, "Does this display tell us about our data in a clear way?" Brainstorm better ways to organize the data, such as a table, tally marks, or a bar graph.

On the board or chart paper, draw lines to make sections for each of the selected ways to prepare potatoes, and label the sections. Ask the students to transfer their drawings to the appropriate section on the new chart (see fig. 2.2). With the class, count the number of squares in each section, and circle any groups of ten that appear in the same section (see fig. 2.3). Record the number of squares in each section. Discuss the newer display. Ask, "Does this chart display the data in a clear way?"

Ask the children to represent the data in a different form. Have them work in groups of two to four students, using readily available materials to make their displays. They can fold index cards in half to label each kind of cooked potato. You might consider assigning different materials to each group. Some groups of children may need guidance. Encourage them to make a graph or chart that makes sense to them and that they think will communicate the information to anyone who looks at their display. Various kinds of displays that the groups might make are illustrated in fig. 2.4a–e.

After the students have created their representations of the data, discuss how their graphs or charts are alike and how they are different: "What is the same about these graphs?" (Some are bar graphs; they tell us about the same data.) "What is different about them?" (They look different: some have numbers, and some don't; some have pictures, and some don't; the data are represented by different materials; one is horizontal, and two are vertical; the labels are in different positions—top, bottom, side—for each graph.) If some students have used numbers in their displays and others have not, discuss these differences with the class.

The children will probably be able to read and interpret the display. The questions you ask, however, should help the students realize that other ways of displaying the data may be clearer.

"Students' representations should be discussed, shared with classmates, and valued because they reflect the students' understandings. These representations afford teachers opportunities to assess students' understandings and to initiate class discussions...." (NCTM 2000, p. 112)

Fig. **2.2.**
Displaying data on a chart

Fig. **2.3.**
Groups of ten circled on a chart

Ask the children how they might change the data display from one form to another, such as from a vertical bar graph to a horizontal bar graph. With such physical models as bars of linked cubes, it is easy to reorient the bars and the corresponding labels (see figs. 2.4b and 2.5). Discuss which type of graph, table, or chart the students think shows

Favorite Kinds of Cooked Potatoes

Mashed Potatoes	(3 sticky notes)
French Fries	(13 sticky notes)
Potato Chips	(4 sticky notes)

(a) A horizontal picture graph with data drawn on sticky notes

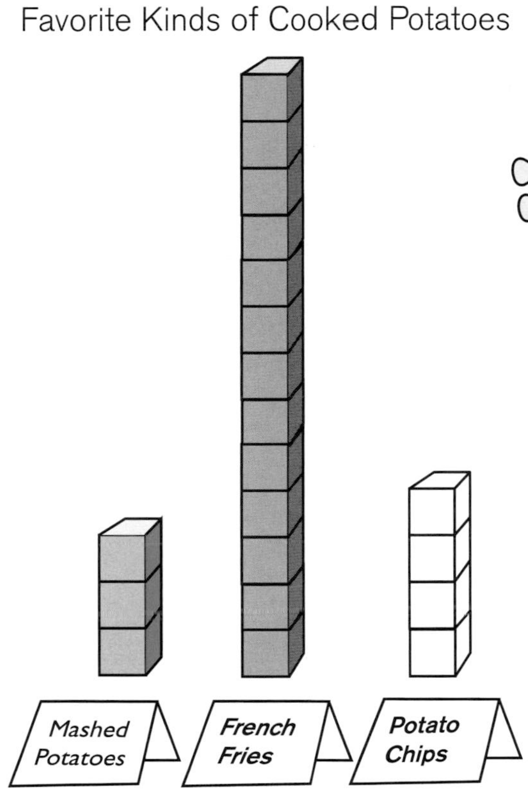

Favorite Kinds of Cooked Potatoes

Mashed Potatoes *French Fries* *Potato Chips*

(b) A vertical bar graph with cubes representing data

Favorite Kinds of Cooked Potatoes

Mashed Potatoes French Fries Potato Chips

(c) A vertical object graph with clothes pins representing data

<table>
<tr><th colspan="2">Favorite Kinds of Cooked Potatoes</th></tr>
<tr><td>Mashed Potatoes</td><td>|||</td></tr>
<tr><td>French Fries</td><td>𝍸 𝍸 |||</td></tr>
<tr><td>Potato Chips</td><td>||||</td></tr>
</table>

(d) A tally chart

Favorite Kinds of Cooked Potatoes	
Mashed Potatoes	3
French Fries	13
Potato Chips	4

(e) A frequency chart

Fig. **2.4.**

Different ways of displaying the same data

Fig. **2.5.**

A horizontal bar graph with cubes representing data

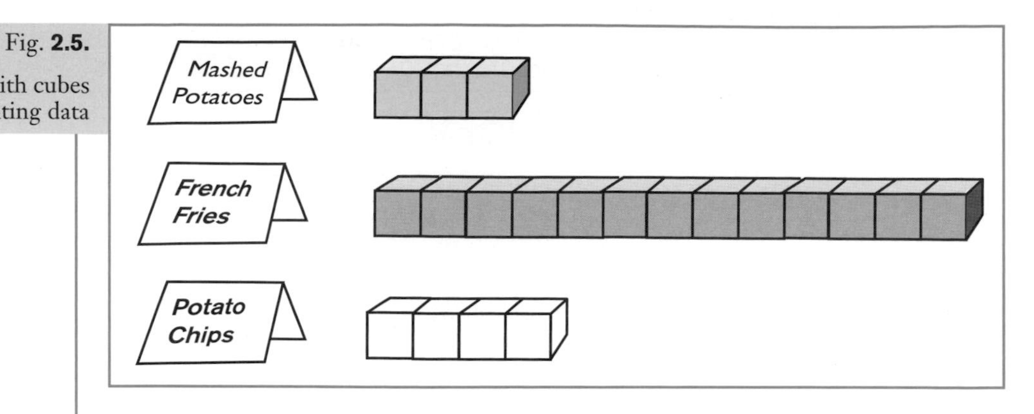

the information most clearly. Ask, “Why did you choose that one? Does anyone have a different choice?”

Extend

Have the children make number sentences using the data from the graphic or symbolic representations (see fig. 2.6). Record the equations and inequalities on the board or on a chart, and make a statement about the potatoes that goes with each expression. For example, $3 < 13$ might correspond to the statement that fewer students prefer mashed potatoes than prefer french fries. The expression $13 - 3 = 10$ might go with the statement that ten more students prefer french fries than prefer mashed potatoes. Discuss whether the expressions relate to all the displays of the data or only to some of them. Lead the students to the realization that all the displays show the same information but in different formats.

Fig. **2.6.**

Number sentences representing the data in the graphical displays

$3 < 13$

$13 > 4$

$4 > 3$

$3 + 13 = 16$

$3 + 4 > 3$

$3 + 13 + 4 = 20$

$13 - 4 = 9$

$$\begin{array}{r} 13 \\ -\ 3 \\ \hline 10 \end{array}$$

$$\begin{array}{r} 13 \\ +\ 4 \\ \hline 17 \end{array}$$

Discussion

The emphasis in Back and Forth is on helping children see that the same data can be displayed in different types of graphs and charts. They can quite literally go “back and forth” between a tally chart and a bar graph or between a horizontal and a vertical bar graph. The focus is not on beautiful displays but rather on becoming involved in *using different ways* to convey information. By constructing their own graphs, students become more engaged with the data, so they learn more about how charts or graphs that look different can display the same data.

The computer helps children represent data in various forms of graphs with very little effort. A computer-generated bar graph of the data on students' favorite kinds of cooked potatoes is shown in figure 2.7. Many computer graphing tools, such as the Graph Club (Sterns 1998), make it easy for children to choose how to represent their data. With the press of a key or mouse, they can transfer data from a table to a picture graph, a chart, or a bar graph.

The applet Get Organized, on the CD-ROM, can be used to extend the idea of representing data in a variety of ways.

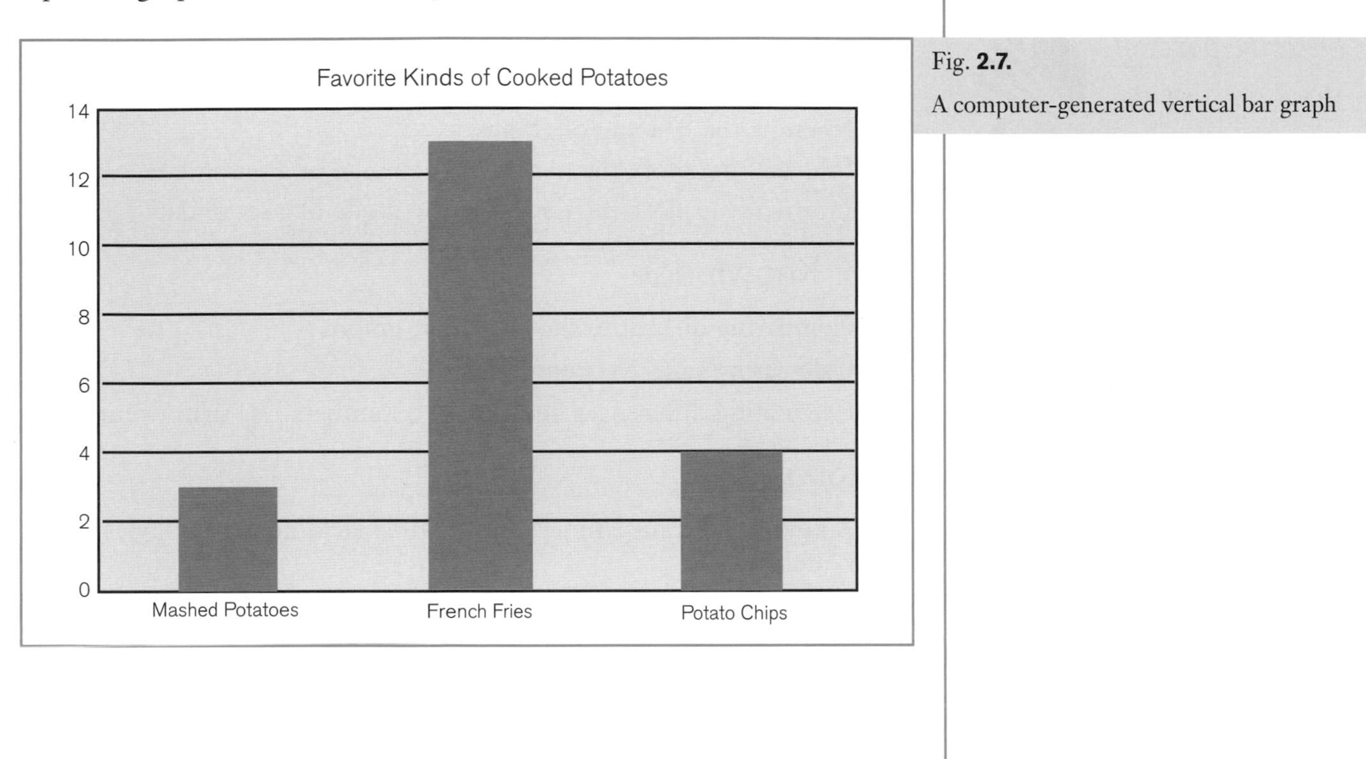

Fig. **2.7.**

A computer-generated vertical bar graph

Mystery Graphs

Grades 1–2

Summary

Given various situations and graphs depicting data associated with those situations, students match the situations to the graphs.

Goals

Describe parts of the data and the set of data as a whole to determine what the data show

- Interpret graphs of data
- Make inferences from graphs of data
- Examine the labeling of graphs
- Informally explore the notion of the range of a set of data
- Informally explore the notion of the mode of a set of data

Prior Knowledge

- Comparing quantities shown on bar graphs
- Calculating sums to twenty
- Calculating differences between two numbers less than twenty

Materials

pp. 83, 84, 85

- An overhead transparency copy of the blackline master "Mystery Graphs"
- A copy of the blackline master "Which Is Which?" for each student
- A copy of the blackline master "More than One Story" for each student
- Scissors
- Paste or tape
- An overhead projector
- Three graphs that students created earlier in the year
- One sheet of one-half-inch grid paper (available on the CD-ROM) for each pair of students
- One slip of paper for each pair of students

Activity

Engage

Begin by asking the students to name some places where they would see more children than adults. Display the transparency copy of "Mystery Graphs" on the overhead projector. Indicate that one of the bar graphs shows the number of adults in a second-grade class and the number of children in the class. The other bar graph shows the number of students in a second-grade class who are six years old and the number of students who are seven years old. Call on a student to indicate which graph is which and to explain why she or he thinks so. Focus on the clues the students used to help them decide which graph is which.

Discuss with the class how the graphs should be titled and labeled. Add a title at the top of each graph; for example, the first one might be titled "People in a Second-Grade Class" and the second, "Ages of Students in a Second-Grade Class." Then add labels for each column—for example, "Adults" and "Children" for the first graph and "Six Years Old" and "Seven Years Old" for the second graph.

Discuss the following questions with the children:

- What do the heights of the bars tell them? (The heights of the bars indicate the number of people in each category.)
- Can they tell the ages of the children and the adult from the left-hand graph? (They cannot.)
- Which bar is the highest in each graph, and why?
- Why are there only two categories in each situation?
- How can they tell the total number of children in the class from each graph? (They can count the squares in the second column in the left-hand graph and add the number of squares in the columns in the right-hand graph.)

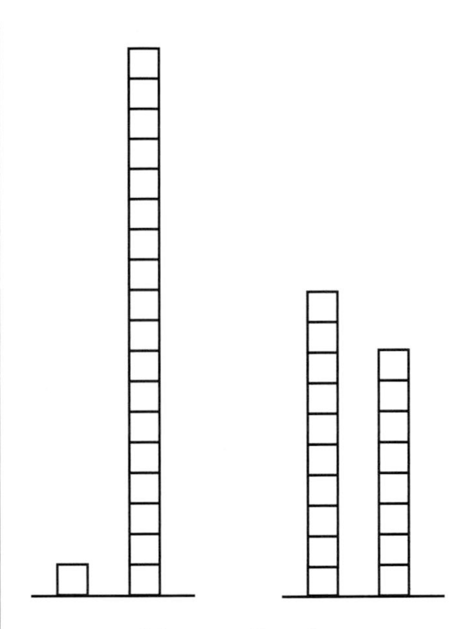
Mystery Graphs

Explore

Remove the titles from three graphs that the students in the class created earlier in the year, and display the graphs. List the titles of all three graphs on the chalkboard. Call on students to match the titles to the graphs and identify the clues they used to help them decide which title goes with which graph. Then restore the titles, and discuss how the graphs differ in the number and names of categories, the heights of the bars, and the distribution of the data. This part of the activity is also appropriate for use in a learning center.

Distribute a copy of "Which Is Which?" to each student. Have the students cut out the titles at the bottom of the sheet and paste or tape each title above the appropriate graph and then label the axes of each graph and the bars in graph C. The labels should be consistent with the title of the graph. Each student should then explain to a partner why his or her titles and labels make sense. Call on some students to give their explanations to the entire class. Have some students tell the class which title they found easiest to determine and explain why.

Ask these additional questions:

- Why are there more categories for graph A than for the other graphs? (There are many moms, and their ages are very spread out. So the moms' ages have been broken down into groups.)
- How many people are in the family represented by graph B? How many children are in the family? (five people, three children)
- How many people were involved in each survey? (A. 23; B. 5; C. 16; D. 23)
- Which category in each graph occurred most often? Why?

Next distribute a copy of "More than One Story" to each student. Have the students look at the graph on the left of the page and tell what they can find out from the graph. Point out that the heights of the bars on the right-hand graph are exactly the same as those on the left-hand graph. Elicit from the students that they do not know what story the graph on the right of the page tells them. Have the students make up a different story to explain the data, and remind them to create a title that makes sense for those data. For example, the story might be about house colors on a given street, with the labels for the tall columns white and red and for the others orange, blue, and green. The students should give a rationale for their title and labels.

Extend

Have the students work in pairs to create a mystery graph on graph paper. On a separate slip of paper—not on the graph—the students should record a title for the graph and appropriate labels for the axis. Have the students write their initials on the backs of both the graph and the paper with the title and labels. Place the graphs in a pile. Separate the title-label papers so the students can see all of them (see the examples in fig. 2.8). Call on students to select a graph and decide which title and labels might match it. Have the students compare their matches with the intent of the creators by checking for matching initials.

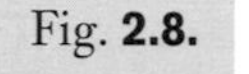

Fig. **2.8.**

Examples of a mystery graph and of students' titles and labels. Only two matches are appropriate.

People Who Like or Don't Like Spaghetti

Like | Do Not Like

Favorite Fruits

Apples | Bananas | Grapes

Ages of Students in Our Class

Seven | Eight

Discussion

The interpretation of graphs is as important as the creation of graphs. Students must look for the clues that help them see that a particular graph fits a particular set of data. They must attend to what the categories are, the number of categories, and the likely frequency of the occurrence of particular categories. Also important, of course, is the correct use of titles and labels, which receives a significant amount of attention in this activity.

The task More than One Story in the "Explore" section focuses students' attention on the concept that the same data may describe any number of different situations. Also, writing stories for the data presented in graphs facilitates the development of students' writing skills.

Conducting a Survey

Grades 1–2

Summary

Students formulate and refine questions and then conduct a survey in order to answer the questions.

Goals

- Formulate and refine questions
- Collect data
- Organize and display data
- Analyze and interpret data

Prior Knowledge

- Collecting and displaying data

Materials

- Materials for displaying data (e.g., paper, sticky notes, linking cubes, chain links, crayons, grid paper)
- A copy of the blackline master "Our Survey" for each pair of students
- One-half-inch grid paper (available on the CD-ROM)
- A large piece of paper (optional)

Activity

Engage

Ask the students to explain what a *preference* is. Once the students understand the term, have them identify some of their own preferences. Record their responses on the board or on a large piece of paper. Allow the students several minutes for brainstorming their preferences, and then ask them if they notice any categories (e.g., food, leisure activities, colors) into which their responses might be sorted.

Tell the students that big companies sometimes spend a lot of time and money to find out about people's preferences. Ask them to talk about why companies might do that.

Explore

Have the students imagine that they have been hired to find out about their classmates' preferences. Tell them that a local bakery is planning to make cookies for a school party and to sell refreshments at a school picnic. Ask, "What would the bakery like to know? Why?" Discuss the importance of asking good questions. The students should test their questions on several classmates to be sure that the questions elicit the answers that they are interested in and that can be easily organized and displayed. Working in pairs, the students should then decide what question to ask and how to collect and display the data. Explain that the students will also be expected to complete a form

"The main purpose of collecting data is to answer questions when the answers are not immediately obvious. Students' natural inclination to ask questions must be nurtured.... Students also should begin to refine their questions to get the information they need."
(NCTM 2000, p. 109)

p. 86

("Our Survey") about their data collection and display and about their findings. Make available the display materials for the students to use.

Allow time for the students to collect and display their data, complete "Our Survey," and present their displays and findings. Discuss the similarities and differences among the questions posed and the ways in which the data were displayed. You may want to create an "Our Preferences" bulletin board where the displays can be exhibited.

Extend

It is important that students recognize the usefulness of mathematics in a variety of careers and businesses. If the students have parents or friends who work in marketing or advertising, you may want to invite them to your class to talk to the students about their work. If such an expert is not available, you may want to make a bulletin board with advertisements that contain such statements as "More dentists prefer...." Such examples help to illustrate the variety of products and services that use data about preferences.

Discussion

"When children are allowed to follow their own interests, they are more motivated to represent their work, even if doing so is difficult." (Dacey and Eston 1999, p. 139)

Students have a natural curiosity that can be nourished by asking them to create their own questions and displays. Having them write their own questions encourages them to choose a question that is meaningful and interesting to them.

As students collect their data, their questions sometimes undergo a natural revision process. For example, if just yes-or-no responses are given, the students may choose to revise their original question from "Do you like cookies?" to "What kinds of cookies do you like?" Similarly, some students may choose to revise their questions in order to make the data they collect easier to organize and display. For example, one pair of students began with the question "What cookies do you like?" When their classmates began to give multiple responses, they narrowed the question to "What kind of cookie is your favorite—chocolate chip, peanut butter, or oatmeal?"

What a Difference a Day Makes

Grades 1–2

Summary

Students are presented with picture graphs with current data. Their job is to decide if each of the graphs would look the same if it displayed data gathered the next day. Students then identify data that will stay the same and those that will change, necessitating a different graph. They follow the same procedure for events occurring "next week," "next month," and "next year."

Develop and evaluate inferences and predictions that are based on data.
(NCTM 2000, p. 108)

Goals

- Describe parts of data displayed in graphs
- Predict which data will be the same or different in one day, one week, one month, or one year

Prior Knowledge

- Reading and interpreting picture graphs

Materials

- Graphs displaying various characteristics of the students or of other first- or second-grade students
- A copy of the blackline master "About Students" for each student
- A copy of the blackline master "More about Students" for each student

pp. 87, 88

Activity

Engage

Distribute a copy of the blackline master "About Students." Use these graphs or ones that show data for the students in your class. Ask questions like the following:

- How many students answered the sock-color question? (23) How can you tell from the graph? (I counted all the smiley faces.)
- Which color of socks are most students wearing? (white) How do you know? (White has the most smiley faces.)
- Which color of socks are the fewest students wearing? (We can't tell.) Why not? (We don't know what colors are represented by the "Other" category.)
- Imagine that you made a graph of the colors of socks for the same students on the day after this graph was made. Would the graph look the same? (probably not) Why? (Most students do not wear socks of the same color every day.)

Follow the same line of questioning for the other graphs. For the pets graph you might also ask these questions:

- Is the number of students who have one pet the same as the number who have two or more pets? (yes)
- How do you know that this is true? (There are eight smiley faces for one pet and also eight smiley faces (2 + 3 + 1 + 2 = 8) for two, three, four, and more than four pets.)

For the ages graph, you might add the following questions:

- What age has the fewest children? (five and eight)
- How will the distribution of ages look next year? (The distribution will move up one year.)
- What age will have the fewest children next year on this date if the same children respond to the questions? (six and nine)

Note that for the ages of students, the graph for the next day would be different only if one or more students had a birthday on the second day. For lunch drinks, the graph for the next day might or might not be the same because, like socks, drinks are the daily choice of the students and thus can vary from day to day. The number of pets and the students' ages, however, are not daily choices and thus are not likely to vary as much.

It is important that you ask the students to explain their reasoning for their answers to these questions. Most students will personalize their answers. For example, if a student in your class always wears white socks, he might think that all other students always wear the same color as well. Or if a student has a pet that recently had babies, she might think that the numbers of other people's pets are also likely to change.

Explore

Distribute a copy of the blackline master "More about Students" to each student. Use the graphs displayed or ones that show data for the students in your class. Pose questions like those for the graph "About Students," but ask if the graphs would look the same the next week or next month—for example, "How will the distribution of heights look next year if all the same children are surveyed?" (Answers may vary. Since children grow at different rates, the distribution in the height graph will probably change.)

Talk about why the graphs would or would not change over various periods of time. For example, students should be able to explain why the height graph would not change in a day or a week but would change over a year. They should understand that a graph of the number of letters in the first names of the students in a class would never change unless new students were admitted, some students left, or a student changed his or her name. They should know that the weather graph might change every day. You might also ask the students to identify which graphs would be different if the data were gathered from another class of the same grade level in your school.

"[Students] should discuss when conclusions about data from one population might or might not apply to data from another population."
(NCTM 2000, p. 109)

Extend

To extend this activity, take another look at the graphs "About Students" and "More about Students." Have the students pose questions about the graphs for their classmates to answer. Discuss which graphs would look the same the next year with data from the same students and which graphs might represent students from classes at different schools and in different grades. Ask the students to think of other information that could be graphed, and discuss which graphs would look the same at different times. Choose a question about some area of interest to the students, such as height or age, and graph answers to the question today, one week from today, and one month from today. Compare the graphs to see what has changed and what has remained the same. Ask another teacher who has students approximately the same age as yours to graph the same data at the same times, and compare the results. You might even use the Internet to share data with a class in another state or country.

Discussion

Graph interpretation is a complex topic for children. In fact, many adults have difficulty interpreting complex graphs. Starting with graphs that contain data about familiar topics is the key to understanding the process. Students will have little trouble understanding that a sock-color graph would not remain static over time, because they know that their socks are not always the same. They may, however, have difficulty with data that do not directly relate to their daily lives. For example, students in a large school with stable enrollment may not realize that a graph showing the number of students in each grade in another school would probably be the same (or close to the same) in different months of a particular school year but would probably not be the same in a different school year. Individual interviews with students are an excellent way to assess their understanding of this complex topic.

Whom Do You Believe?

Grade 2

Summary

Given a data set and two different interpretations of the data, students talk about which interpretation to believe. Data are shown in various ways, including in misleading bar graphs with units of different sizes.

"Misconceptions that arise because of students' representations of data offer situations for new learning and instruction."
(NCTM 2000, p. 112)

Goals

- Identify misrepresentations of data
- Read and interpret picture graphs in which the pictures represent more than one individual

Prior Knowledge

- Reading and interpreting bar graphs
- Reading and interpreting picture graphs in which each picture stands for one item

Materials

pp. 89, 90

- Small blue cubes, medium-sized red cubes, large yellow cubes (Paper squares of different sizes and different colors may be substituted.)
- One-half-inch grid paper (available on the CD-ROM)
- A copy of the blackline master "Favorite Colors" to distribute or for use on the overhead projector
- A transparency copy of "Children in a Class" for use on the overhead projector
- An overhead projector

Activity

Engage

Show the students a pile of small blue cubes, medium-sized red cubes, and large yellow cubes. Ask the students one by one to pick a cube in their favorite color. After all the students have chosen cubes, ask them to put the cubes in three piles—one for each color—so that everyone can see the piles. Ask the students which color of cube is the most popular in the class. Encourage the students to look carefully at the piles of cubes but not to move them or even touch them.

The students might disagree about which color is the most popular. Some students might base their answer on the size of the pile without noticing that the differences in the sizes of the cubes may account for the differences in the sizes of the piles. Ask the students if they can think of a better way to tell which color is the most popular. Try some of the students' suggestions. If they do not suggest putting cubes of the same color in a row or column to form a bar graph, you might remind them of some of their earlier work using bar graphs to organize and analyze data.

Explore

After the children have worked with cubes as a class, distribute copies of "Favorite Colors" or display a transparency copy on the overhead projector. Tell the students that this graph was made from data gathered from another class. Together, read Tara and Judy's discussion of the meaning of the graph. Ask the children whether they believe Tara is correct or Judy is correct. How could they confirm their choices? Solicit a variety of suggestions, and follow up on the most promising ideas by having the students carry out their suggestions. For example, the students may suggest getting colored cubes of the same size and building the graphs with actual cubes. Or they might suggest using grid paper and coloring the columns of squares to match the colors indicated in "Favorite Colors."

Extend

Once the students understand that bar graphs are misleading if the scale for the bars does not remain constant, display "Children in a Class" on the overhead projector. Before revealing the comments from Dan and Jon, show the students the picture graph and the key that indicates the number of people represented by each picture (smiley face). Ask the students whether they believe there are more girls or more boys in this class. Encourage them to give reasons for their answers, and then show them Dan's and Jon's responses. Ask them whether they believe that Jon or Dan is correct. Compare the students' reasoning with Dan's and Jon's reasoning.

Call on students to suggest better ways to represent the number of students in the class. If they suggest using the small smiley face always to represent two children, ask them how they would represent the fifteen boys. If the students have not used pictographs in which fractions of a picture are used to represent fewer items than the full picture represents, you might suggest using "half a face" for one child. Have the students create their own pictographs to represent the children in Dan and Jon's class or in their own class, and then compare pictographs. Check that all the pictures represent the same information accurately. Have the students talk about which pictures might be better to use than others. Ask them if it matters whether one face stands for two, three, four, or five students.

Discussion

This activity gives students early experiences that demonstrate the importance of scale and choice of unit. With the actual objects and with the bar graphs, students begin to grapple with problems that arise when the sizes of the objects, the bars, or the pictures are not consistent. Encouraging students to discuss their different interpretations of the graphs gives you an opportunity to assess whether they have misunderstandings about the data representations. Some students may need several experiences with different representations before they begin to understand how data can be misrepresented. The ability to recognize and interpret varying representations of data will serve students throughout their lives as they analyze data to make everyday decisions. As the students gain more experience with these ideas, they might be interested in discussing whether data are ever intentionally

Favorite Colors

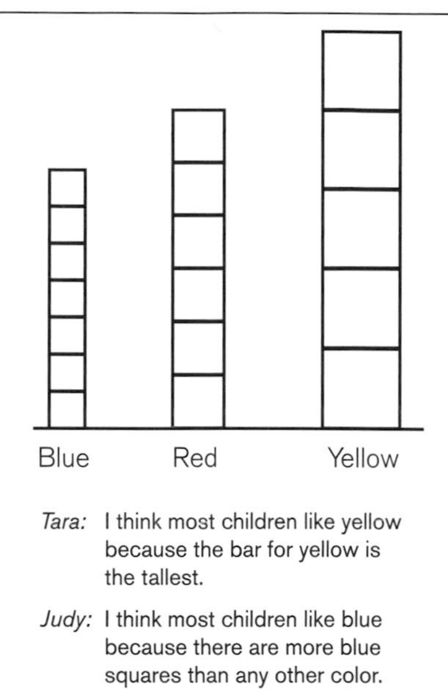

Tara: I think most children like yellow because the bar for yellow is the tallest.

Judy: I think most children like blue because there are more blue squares than any other color.

Children in a Class

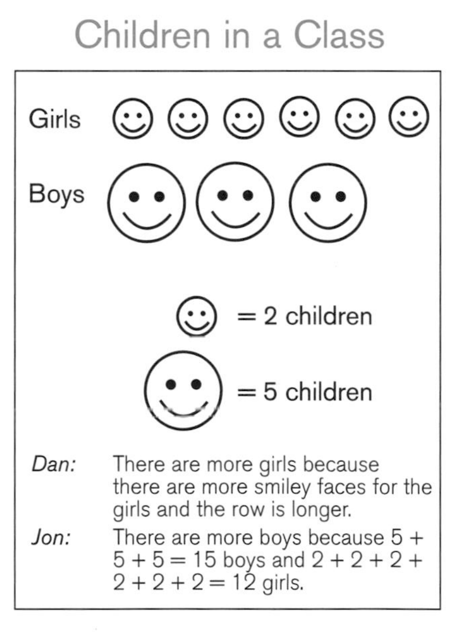

Dan: There are more girls because there are more smiley faces for the girls and the row is longer.

Jon: There are more boys because 5 + 5 + 5 = 15 boys and 2 + 2 + 2 + 2 + 2 + 2 = 12 girls.

"By the end of grade 2, students should begin to question inappropriate statements about data." (NCTM 2000, p. 113)

misleading. Different politicians and different advertisers often use the same data to support very different claims; some students might be ready to discuss such issues.

Using a single picture to represent more than one object might be a new idea for the students. Interesting conversations arise as they explore how to use part of a picture to represent fewer objects than are represented by an entire picture. You might want to take advantage of this opportunity to tie the lesson on graphing to one on fractions or symmetry. Deciding how to represent fifteen children when each picture stands for two children or how to represent twelve children when each picture stands for five children allows students to use what they know about division, working with parts of wholes, and choosing shapes that can easily be partitioned.

Travel Agent

Grade 2

Summary

Students are given pertinent information about three possible class trips as well as the results of a survey about a class's preferences. On the basis of the survey data and the information about the possible destinations, students must choose the trip that is most suitable for the class, and they must justify their choice.

Goals

- Analyze relevant data to answer questions
- Use data to justify choices

Prior Knowledge

- Finding information in a table
- Adding whole-dollar amounts of money
- Combining lengths of time

Materials

- A copy of the two-page blackline master "Class Trip" for each student
- Drawing materials for producing a "travel brochure" or advertisement

Activity

Engage

Give each student a copy of "Class Trip." Together, read about the choices for trips. Answer any questions that might arise about the trips and the information known about getting there, the amount of time spent at the site, the bus and entrance fees, and the choices of things to do while at the site.

When all the questions have been answered, read and discuss the results of a survey of a class on the second page of "Class Trip." Again answer questions that may arise. At this point, the students should work on their own to act as the "travel agent" for that class. They must decide, using the results of the survey, which of the three trips is best suited to that class.

Explore

After all the students have made their decisions, arrange the students in small groups of three or four. The groups must discuss the individuals' choices and then come to a common decision. Tell the groups that they must be able to justify their choice to the rest of the class. If a group is having difficulty reaching a decision, suggest that each member give some reasons why his or her choice is best. After the students discuss their reasons, the group may be able to reach a consensus. If

"Through data investigations, teachers should encourage students to think clearly and to check new ideas against what they already know in order to develop concepts for making informed decisions."
(NCTM 2000, p. 109)

p. 91

not, then they may present two reports to the class reflecting the differences of opinion in the group.

Have each group or subgroup prepare a report to present to the class. In the report, the students should give at least three reasons why their choice is the best. They must present data to back up their claims. You might suggest that they think of the report as a newspaper or TV advertisement about the trip. After all the groups have given their reports, have the whole class vote on the most suitable trip and give their reasons in the form of an advertisement about the trip.

Extend

To extend this activity, have the students gather information on possible field trips. The students should first decide what information they need about the trips and what questions they would ask in a survey to determine their preferences. Remind them that they must decide the best ways to organize the data that they collect. After information has been collected about several sites in your area and the students have responded to the survey, repeat the parts of the activity in the "Engage" and "Explore" sections, using the class's data. If your class takes a yearly field trip, you might arrange for the students to take the trip that they choose.

Discussion

The primary purpose of this activity is to help students understand how to use data to make decisions. In this exercise, it is particularly important that the students understand that the decisions must be based on the data, not on their own likes and dislikes. Since several factors are involved, the students must decide which factors are more important and which are less important.

This activity presents an opportunity for students to begin to "learn how to keep track of multiple responses to their questions and those posed by others. Students also should begin to refine their questions to get the information they need" (NCTM 2000, p. 109).

You should expect great diversity in students' performance on this activity. Some of the groups may have idiosyncratic reasons for their choices, whereas others may surprise you with the precision of their thinking. Let the students discuss their choices in small groups as much as possible. This activity may take more than one day.

Conclusion

The first two chapters focused on collecting, organizing, and displaying data and on posing questions and analyzing data. In chapter 3, the emphasis is on simple, introductory probability concepts.

PRE-K–GRADE 2

DATA ANALYSIS *and* PROBABILITY

Chapter 3
Probability

The activities in this chapter introduce students to simple ideas about probability, such as likely or unlikely events. The activities focus on decisions students make on the basis of their experiences or the data they collect in simple experiments. Students in prekindergarten–grade 2 are familiar with probability ideas from their everyday experiences. They may have heard the weather analyst on television talk about the chance that it will rain, and they might hear their parents discuss the likelihood that the next phone call will be from Grandma. They may have rolled dice or spun spinners when playing games.

The probability of the occurrence of events is defined by the equation

$$\text{Probability} = \frac{\text{Number of ways that an event of interest can occur}}{\text{Number of ways that all events can occur}}.$$

For instance, the probability of getting an even number when a regular six-sided die is rolled is found by dividing the number of ways an even number can occur (there are three ways: 2, 4, 6) by the total number of numbers on the die, or 6. Therefore, the probability of getting an even number is 3/6, which can be reduced to 1/2.

Young students should be introduced to correct vocabulary as they learn simple probability concepts. Some of the terms that they should learn include the following:

- *Certain event*—an event that will always happen
- *Equally likely events*—events (such as the outcomes of an experiment) that have the same chance of occurring

- *Fair game*—a game in which all players have an equal chance of winning
- *Impossible event*—an event that has no chance of happening
- *Likely event*—an event that will probably happen
- *Possible event*—an event that has a chance of happening
- *Predict*—to tell what might happen in the future
- *Random sample*—a sample drawn from a population in such a way that each individual has an equal chance of being chosen.
- *Sample space*—the set of all possible outcomes for an experiment
- *Unlikely event*—something that will probably not happen

It is important for students to recognize that on a scale from "impossible" to "certain," "possible" is between the two extremes (see fig. 3.1). As students become more familiar with probability, the scale can be modified to replace the verbal descriptors with numerals: "certain" indicates a probability of 1 and "impossible" indicates a probability of 0.

Fig. **3.1.**

A scale showing the relationships among probabilities expressed verbally

Possible

Impossible Unlikely Likely Certain

You can use the simulated spinners and dice in the applet Probability Games, on the CD-ROM, to replicate some of the games in this chapter.

In Spin It, students use simple probability ideas to predict the likelihood of a spinner's coming to rest on different colors on backgrounds that have varying areas of the colors. Students predict the colors of the cubes in a bag from samples drawn from the bag in the activity Which Bag Is Which? Building on their knowledge of their environments and what they know is likely or unlikely to occur, students examine the likelihood of everyday events in Possible or Impossible. In Some Sums, students make organized lists to analyze data and make simple predictions on the basis of their analyses. The actual calculation of mathematical probability is introduced in later grades.

Expectations for Students' Accomplishment

By the end of grade 2, students should understand simple probability concepts and correctly use the vocabulary to describe such ideas as likely, unlikely, possible, and impossible. They should have played simple games using spinners and dice and should be able to discuss whether the games are fair. It may be several more years before students are ready to formalize these elementary probability concepts and calculate exact mathematical probabilities; during these early years, however, students should record and analyze informal experimental results.

Possible or Impossible

Prekindergarten–Kindergarten

Summary

Students investigate the likelihood that certain events in their imaginations, in their lives, and in literature will occur, and they make drawings of what is possible and impossible for them to do.

Goals

- Identify the likelihood of events

Prior Knowledge

- Familiarity with the terms *possible* and *impossible*

Materials

- A book of nursery rhymes or a storybook
- Drawing materials: crayons, paints, paper

Activity

Engage

Talk about characters and events that are possible or impossible, drawing from students' imaginations and books, rhymes, children's television shows, and familiar videotapes or current movies.

Explore

Copy the chart in figure 3.2a onto the board, and read nursery rhymes such as "Hickory, Dickory, Dock" and "Hey, Diddle, Diddle" to the children (see fig. 3.3). Reread the nursery rhymes line by line and have the class decide in which category in the chart—"possible" or "impossible"—each line should be placed. An example is shown in figure 3.2b.

Extend

Extend the discussion to actions that are possible for the students to do and actions that are impossible for them to do. Have the students make drawings of what they cannot do and what they can do. Display their drawings on the bulletin board under columns labeled "Possible" and "Impossible." Discuss which of these classifications may change when the students get older.

Discussion

This activity uses literature with which young children are generally familiar to focus on the likelihood of events. The students may disagree about the likelihood of some of the events, such as "the little dog laughed." These differences of opinion should be discussed.

Older students and adults may be familiar with other meanings of nursery rhymes. "Hey, Diddle, Diddle" is sometimes said to be a story about the stars, with the dog as Sirius, the Dog Star, and the spoon as

"Questions about more and less likely events should come from the students' experiences, and the answers will often depend on the community and its location." (NCTM 2000, p. 114)

Fig. **3.2.**
Probability charts

Possible	Impossible

(a) A blank probability chart

Possible	Impossible
The mouse ran up the clock.	The cow jumped over the moon.
The clock struck one.	The dish ran away with the spoon.
The mouse ran down.	
The cat and the fiddle,	
The little dog laughed	

(b) A probability chart filled out for "Hickory, Dickory, Dock" and "Hey, Diddle, Diddle"

Fig. **3.3.**
Two nursery rhymes

Hickory, Dickory, Dock

Hickory, dickory, dock,
The mouse ran up the clock.
The clock struck one.
The mouse ran down.
Hickory, dickory, dock.

Hey, Diddle, Diddle

Hey, diddle, diddle,
The cat and the fiddle,
The cow jumped over the moon.
The little dog laughed
To see such sport,
And the dish ran away with the spoon.

the Big Dipper. Others say the animals represent misbehaving members of the royal court of Queen Elizabeth I! Young students, however, think about the literal meanings of the rhymes, and this concrete focus presents teachers and studenets with opportunities to consider the likelihood of the descriptions and events.

Spin It

Grades K–1

Summary

After a discussion of events that are likely or unlikely, students are shown a spinner with sections of different colors and asked which colors are the most likely to occur. They then play a game in which they spin the spinner and the player who is assigned the indicated color takes a cube of that color. Before spinning, students predict the color that will be indicated most often. They then play several rounds of the game to see if their prediction was correct. The game is repeated with spinners having colored sections of different sizes and then with spinners having different numbers of colors.

Goals

- Identify events that are likely or unlikely
- Compare events in order to decide which are more likely, less likely, and equally likely
- Use a chart to record data

Prior Knowledge

- Recognizing and matching colors
- Counting to ten

Materials

- A copy of the blackline master "Spin It" for each pair of students. The copies can be made on card stock, or they can be made on paper and then mounted on cardboard.
- Crayons or markers
- Paper clips
- Cellophane tape
- A compass or a pen
- Four spinners for each pair of students. To make the spinners, color the sections of the spinners on "Spin It" as indicated. Cut out the spinners. Mount them on cardboard if necessary. Poke a small hole in the center of each spinner using the point of a compass or a sturdy pen. Unbend the end of a paper clip and poke it through the hole from the back. Tape the rest of the paper clip to the back of the cardboard. Put a second paper clip on the protruding end of the first one to use as a needle. Make sure that the paper clip can spin freely. (See the photos in the margin.)
- Ten red and ten blue cubes for each pair of children
- Magazines or children's books

"Teachers should address the beginnings of probability through informal activities with spinners or number cubes that reinforce conceptions in other Standards." *(NCTM 2000, p. 114)*

p. 93

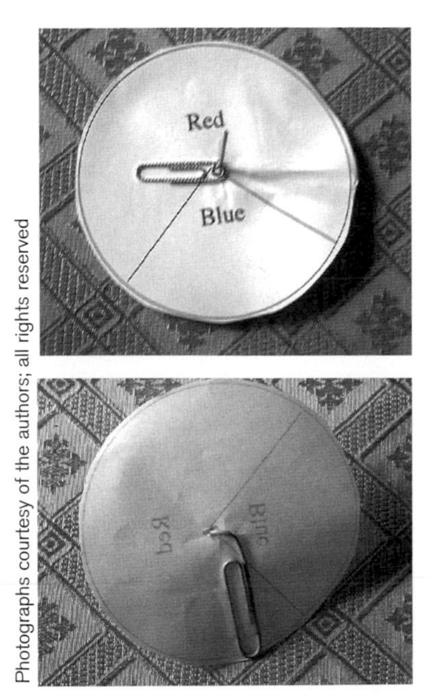

Activity

Engage

Seat the students in a circle and talk about events that they believe are likely to happen tomorrow and events that they believe are unlikely to happen tomorrow. Give each pair of students a magazine or a book and ask them to find pictures that illustrate events that are likely and unlikely to happen to them tomorrow. Have the students share with the group the pictures they have chosen and talk about the reasons for their choices. Then ask them to name the event that they believe is the most likely to happen tomorrow and the one that is the least likely to happen tomorrow. Ask, "Do you believe some of the events are equally likely?"

Explore

Using spinner 1, show the students how the paper clip can be spun to determine a color. Tell them that they will take turns spinning the spinner and taking a cube of the color shown. Ask, "What colors could you get?" "Which color are you more likely to get?" "Which color are you less likely to get?" Play one game as a whole class. Designate half the class to be the blue team and half to be the red team. Call on different students to spin for their team. Regardless of which team is spinning, every time the spinner lands on red, the red team should take a red cube and every time the spinner lands on blue, the blue team should take a blue cube. The first team to collect ten cubes wins.

After the students play as a whole class, have pairs of students play the same game. Designate a red player and a blue player in each pair. Give each pair a spinner, ten red cubes, and ten blue cubes. After all the pairs have played the game, call them back into the circle to discuss their findings. Record the results of their games on a chart like the one in figure 3.4. Ask whether one event occurred more often than the other and why they think it did. (With spinner 1, it is likely that red will have won more times because the red section of the spinner is larger than the blue section.) Ask the students if they believe that this is a "fair" game and why or why not. (This is not a fair game because the red area of the spinner is larger than the blue area, so the spinner is more likely to land on red than on blue.) Ask them to predict the results if they played the game again. (It is more likely that red would win.)

Fig. **3.4.**
A chart for recording the results of the game

Results of the Game Using Spinner 1

Number of times that blue won	
Number of times that red won	
Total number of spins	

Show the students spinner 2. Ask them if they think the results of playing with this spinner will be the same as those of playing with spinner 1 and why they think so. As before, divide the class into pairs; give each pair spinner 2, ten red cubes, and ten blue cubes, and assign one child to be the red player and one to be the blue player. Have them play the game as before, and bring the children together in the circle to record the results, as before. Compare the results of this game with the results of the first game. Ask, "How are the games alike?" "How are the games different?" Talk about why the results might be different. (The red and blue sections of the spinners are different; the sections are equal in spinner 2, so each player has an equal chance of winning; the game is fair. The red section in spinner 1 is larger than the blue section, so the red player has a greater chance of winning; the game is not fair.)

Extend

The students who understand the connection between the areas of the colors on the spinner and the result of the game should be encouraged to play the game again using spinner 3. Ask the students if they think that the results would be similar to or different from the results for spinner 2, and have them give rationales for their answers. Again, record the results of the game on a chart, and compare these results with those for games 1 and 2. Discuss whether the results would be the same if they played each of the games again.

Challenge the students to design a spinner that will help blue win. They can use spinner 4, which is blank, to outline and color their design. They should play the game several times to check whether blue usually wins.

Note that the applet Probability Games, on the CD-ROM, can be used to give students more experiences with spinners and concepts of chance.

After playing these games with two colors, the students may wish to design other spinners that use three or more colors. For games played with such a spinner, the cubes should be the same colors as the colors on the spinner and the number of players (or teams) should be equal to the number of colors. For each design, discuss whether the game would be fair for all players.

Discussion

Preschool children generally have not developed concepts of chance or probability. They might have heard the terms *likely* and *unlikely* used by their parents, but they may not understand the meanings of the words. The students may think that the spinner will land on red because red is their favorite color or that it will land on blue because it landed on red last time and now it is blue's turn. Be sure to talk to the students about the reasons for their predictions. Some students may not be ready to discuss the meaning of *likely* or *unlikely* with any understanding, although this activity might offer those students practice in matching colors and in counting to ten. Allow those students to play the games and notice the different empirical results. The teacher's intent should not be to teach the "correct" way to think about these ideas; such concepts develop naturally over the course of many such experiences and discussions.

"Teachers should encourage students to make conjectures and to justify their thinking empirically or with reasonable arguments."
(NCTM 2000, p. 126)

Which Bag Is Which?

Grades 1–2

Discuss events related to students' experiences as likely or unlikely

Summary

From samples of colored cubes drawn from bags, students predict the predominant color of cubes in the bags.

Goals

- Make predictions from samples
- Compare events to tell which is most likely
- Relate past events to future events

Prior Knowledge

- Comparing quantities less than ten
- Using tally marks to represent objects

Materials

- Three paper bags, each large enough to hold ten colored cubes. Fill the bags as follows:
  - Bag 1: Eight yellow cubes and two blue cubes
  - Bag 2: Five yellow cubes and five blue cubes
  - Bag 3: Two yellow cubes and eight blue cubes
- Twenty red cubes and twenty green cubes for each pair of students
- Two small paper bags (labeled "Bag A" and "Bag B") for each pair of students
- Enough copies of the blackline master "Color Predictions" for each pair of students to have one prediction slip
- Enough copies of the blackline master "Color Splits" for each pair of students to have one color-split square
- Paper and pencils

pp. 95, 96

Activity

Engage

Seat the students in a circle so that they can easily see the colors of the cubes that you draw from the bags. Begin with bag 1. Remove a cube from the bag, record its color, and make a tally mark on a chart similar to the one in the margin. Ask, "What colors are in the bag?" "Could there be other colors in the bag?" "How sure are you?" "Can you tell how many cubes are in the bag without looking in it?"

Blue	II
Yellow	I

Replace the cube in bag 1.Three times, repeat the process of removing a cube, recording its color, and returning it to the bag. Ask the same questions as before about the colors of the cubes in the bag and how sure the students are about their answers. Ask the students which color they think the next cube is more likely to be—blue or yellow—and why. Repeat the exercise six more times so that a total of ten cubes are removed and replaced. Ask the students whether they think there are more yellow cubes or blue cubes in the bag and why they think so.

Repeat the same exercise with bags 2 and 3. Then ask the students from which bag they would draw a cube in order to be more likely to get a yellow one. Call on one student to draw a single cube from the designated bag and note whether it is yellow. Disclose the contents of all three bags. Discuss why the students are more likely to draw a yellow cube from bag 1 than from bag 3.

Explore

Place the students in pairs. Give each pair a paper bag marked "Bag A," ten red cubes, ten green cubes, and one prediction slip from "Color Predictions." Have the students fill their bags with ten cubes, some red and some green, so that their prediction is likely to be true. Then direct the students to complete the experiment (choosing one cube, making a tally mark for its color, returning it to the bag, choosing another cube, tallying its color, returning it to the bag, and so on, until ten cubes have been chosen) to see if the results are as predicted. An example of one pair's tally is shown in figure 3.5. Have the students share their results, and talk about why it might be possible to put different numbers of red cubes in a bag and get similar results.

Fig. **3.5.**

A tally of the colors of cubes drawn from a bag

Anna and tina.

Red and Green equally likely

A.
Red ||||
Green |

T.
Red |
Green ||||

Extend

Give each pair of students bag A and bag B, ten red cubes, ten green cubes, and a square from the blackline master "Color Splits," which indicates the number of red cubes and green cubes to put into each of the two bags. Tell the students that they will be conducting an experiment by removing cubes, one cube at a time, from each bag; recording the colors; and replacing the cubes after each draw.

Before they begin the experiment, they should make a prediction about the results. Record the following five statements on the board. Have the pairs choose which statement is most likely to apply to the situation described by its slip of paper. Read each statement with the students to be sure they understand it.

- Many more red cubes from bag A than from bag B
- Many more red cubes from bag B than from bag A
- A few more red cubes from bag A than from bag B

- A few more red cubes from bag B than from bag A
- The same number of red cubes from both bags

Have the pairs of students perform the experiment by first filling the bags and then selecting, recording, and replacing ten cubes to determine if their predictions are correct.

The students should discuss which circumstances made it easier to predict correctly. For example, the color splits in squares 1 (in which red greatly predominates in both bags) and 11 (in which red predominates in bag 1 and green predominates in bag 2) make it easy to predict correctly. Several of the splits, however, are so close that accurate predictions are difficult to make.

Discussion

This activity helps students begin to understand the concepts of likelihood and of inferring information about a population from a sample. The latter will be examined in much greater detail in later grades.

It is important that students understand that some knowledge is intuitive and that other knowledge comes from experience: Sometimes they can predict events intuitively, and sometimes they must conduct experiments as a basis for making sound predictions. For example, most (but not all) students recognize that a coin is just as likely to come up heads as tails when it is flipped and that if a bag is known to have ten red cubes and one green one, a red cube is more likely to be removed on a draw than a green one. However, we do not understand all situations intuitively, so we must conduct experiments to help us predict events. In some of the situations in this activity, we can predict which event is more likely only after removing many cubes and coming to conclusions about the results. Students should understand that they can predict more accurately after many draws.

Some Sums

Grade 2

Summary

Students gather data on the sums of the numbers that result from tosses of number cubes. They identify the sums that are most and least likely to occur and those that have the same chance of occurring.

Goals

- Conduct experiments to collect data to answer a question
- Organize data in tables
- Identify likely and unlikely events

Prior Knowledge

- Adding single-digit numbers
- Recording numerals through 20
- Identifying odd and even numbers

Materials

- Two cubes of different colors (e.g., red and green), each numbered 1, 1, 2, 2, 3, 3, for each student
- Pencils and lined paper for recording data for each pair of students

Activity

Engage

Review odd and even numbers with the students. Remind them that even numbers are the numbers we say when we count by twos, starting at zero. Odd numbers are the other numbers.

Give each pair of students two number cubes and a record sheet, and have them record the numbers 1 through 20 in a column. Call on students to identify the numbers on the six faces of each cube. Have the students work in pairs to roll the cubes twenty times, each time recording the sum of the numbers on the tops of the cubes as an addition sentence, as shown in figure 3.6. They should list the addends from the cubes in the same order each time (e.g., 1 on red and 2 on green; 2 on red and 1 on green; note that these are different combinations).

When the students have finished, have the pairs identify each sum as odd or even and find the total number of odd sums and the total of even sums. Ask the following questions:

- How can you get a sum that is odd? (With the following combinations: 1, 2; 2, 1; 2, 3; 3, 2)
- How can you get a sum that is even? (With the following combinations: 1, 1; 1, 3; 2, 2; 3, 1; 3, 3)
- If you roll the cubes twenty times again, what do you think you will get—more even sums or more odd sums? Why do you think so?

"At this level, probability experiences should be informal and often take the form of answering questions about the likelihood of events, using such vocabulary as more likely *or* less likely." *(NCTM 2000, p. 114)*

Fig. **3.6.**

A record of the sums of the numbers that resulted from tosses of number cubes

Roll	Cube Sums
1	2 + 3 = 5
2	2 + 2 = 4
3	1 + 1 = 2
4	1 + 2 = 3
5	3 + 2 = 5
6	2 + 2 = 4
7	3 + 3 = 6

It is recommended that you combine data from the entire class to reveal the sums that occur most and least often.

Fig. **3.7.**

A frequency table on which to record the number of times each sum was rolled

Sum	Number of Times Rolled
2	
3	
4	
5	
6	

Explore

Have the pairs of students record their data in a frequency table like that in figure 3.7. Suggest that they lightly cross out each sum in their original charts as it is counted in order to avoid double counting. When they have completed their frequency tables, call on students to identify the sum that occurred most often and the one that occurred least often.

Ask the following questions:

- Is it possible to get a sum of 1? (no) Why? (It is not possible because the smallest number on a cube is 1, and 1 plus 1 is 2.)
- What is the smallest sum you can get? (2)
- What is the greatest sum you can get? (6) When does that happen? (It happens when each cube shows a 3.)
- Think about what you rolled to get each sum. What do you have to roll to get—
    - a sum of 2? (1, 1)
    - a sum of 3? (1, 2 or 2, 1)
    - a sum of 4? (1, 3 or 2, 2 or 3, 1)
    - a sum of 5? (2, 3 or 3, 2)
    - a sum of 6? (3, 3)

Record on the board the pairs of numbers that produce each sum. Then ask the following:

- If you roll the cubes again, which sum are you most likely to get? (4) Why? (There are three ways to get 4 but only two ways to get 3 or 5 and only one way to get 2 or 6.)
- If you roll the cubes again, which sum are you least likely to get? (2 or 6) Why? (There is only one way to get 2 or 6, but there are two or three ways to get the other sums.)

Students might enjoy using the activity Dice Sums in the applet Probability Games, on the CD-ROM, to continue this activity.

Extend

Repeat the same activity using different number cubes, for example, two cubes numbered 1, 2, 2, 3, 3, 3 or two numbered 2, 2, 4, 4, 6, 6.

Discussion

To help students visualize the difference between the result "2 on the first cube, 3 on the second cube" and the result "3 on the first cube, 2 on the second cube," it is recommended that you use cubes of different colors.

The connection between Some Sums and the number strand is clear. Throughout Some Sums, students are adding, partitioning sums to identify pairs of addends, and recording and comparing numbers. They are also gaining familiarity with the commutative property of addition through such examples as that 3 on the first cube and 2 on the second cube produces the same sum as 2 on the first cube and 3 on the second cube. For these reasons, Some Sums can also serve as a maintenance activity for number skills.

As the students work in pairs to conduct the experiments, they will develop their oral communication skills and their abilities to follow directions, share materials, and listen to one another.

Conclusion

Throughout this chapter, activities have been described that help students understand and apply the basic concepts of probability that will serve as a foundation for later learning.

PRE-K–GRADE 2

DATA ANALYSIS *and* PROBABILITY

Looking Back and Looking Ahead

All students develop data sense as they engage in everyday activities. *Navigating through Data Analysis and Probability in Prekindergarten–Grade 2* lays the foundation for working more formally with data, analyzing data, and determining the likelihood of events.

As young students gain experience, they should be able not only to categorize objects into distinct, nonintersecting categories but also to place correctly in a Venn diagram objects that possess zero, one, or two specified attributes. By the end of grade 2, students should be able to sort and classify data according to two intersecting attributes. Some students may even be able to categorize objects using three intersecting categories, such as color, shape, and size, but most children will not have developed that skill until grade 3.

Students should be able to organize and represent data in a variety of ways. By the end of grade 2, they should be able to construct and interpret vertical and horizontal bar graphs, simple line plots, frequency tables with tallies and numbers, two-loop Venn diagrams, and pictographs in which a picture represents two, five, or ten objects. In grades 3–5, students will extend their use of representations to line graphs, three-loop Venn diagrams, and double-bar graphs.

By the end of grade 2, students should also understand that titles and labels are necessary on displays of data so that the information is clearly conveyed. These ideas will be expanded in grades 3–5, when students will also encounter and discuss issues such as why the horizontal axis on a graph should extend to values that are not in the data set and how to represent zero on a graph.

Before they enter grade 3, students should be able to refine questions so that they can gather information appropriate for answering the questions and to keep track of the responses to questions and results of experiments. They should be able to analyze the data collected in order to verify or refute their predictions and answer their questions. Making predictions on the basis of data is informal at this level. More-formal methods of interpreting data will be used in grades 3–5. At that time, students will learn to pay attention to such characteristics of the data set as where the data are concentrated and which data points seem to have unusual values. They will focus on the shape of the data as well as how the data are spread across the range of values, and they will use this information to compare data sets. Students will make conjectures, show how their conjectures are based on data, and design studies to test their conjectures. They will investigate factors that affect the representativeness of a sample.

By the end of grade 2, students should understand simple probability concepts and correctly use the terms *likely*, *unlikely*, *possible*, and *impossible*. They should have had experience with simple games using spinners and dice and should be able to discuss whether the games are fair. Students will most likely not be ready for several years to formalize these elementary probability concepts and calculate exact mathematical probabilities, but during these early years, students should conduct informal experiments and record the results. In grades 3 through 5, they will begin to quantify likelihood and predict the frequency of various outcomes.

PRE-K–GRADE 2

DATA ANALYSIS *and* PROBABILITY

Appendix

Blackline Masters and Solutions

Vertical Graph Mat

Name ______________________________

Draw your group's graph. Add a title and labels.

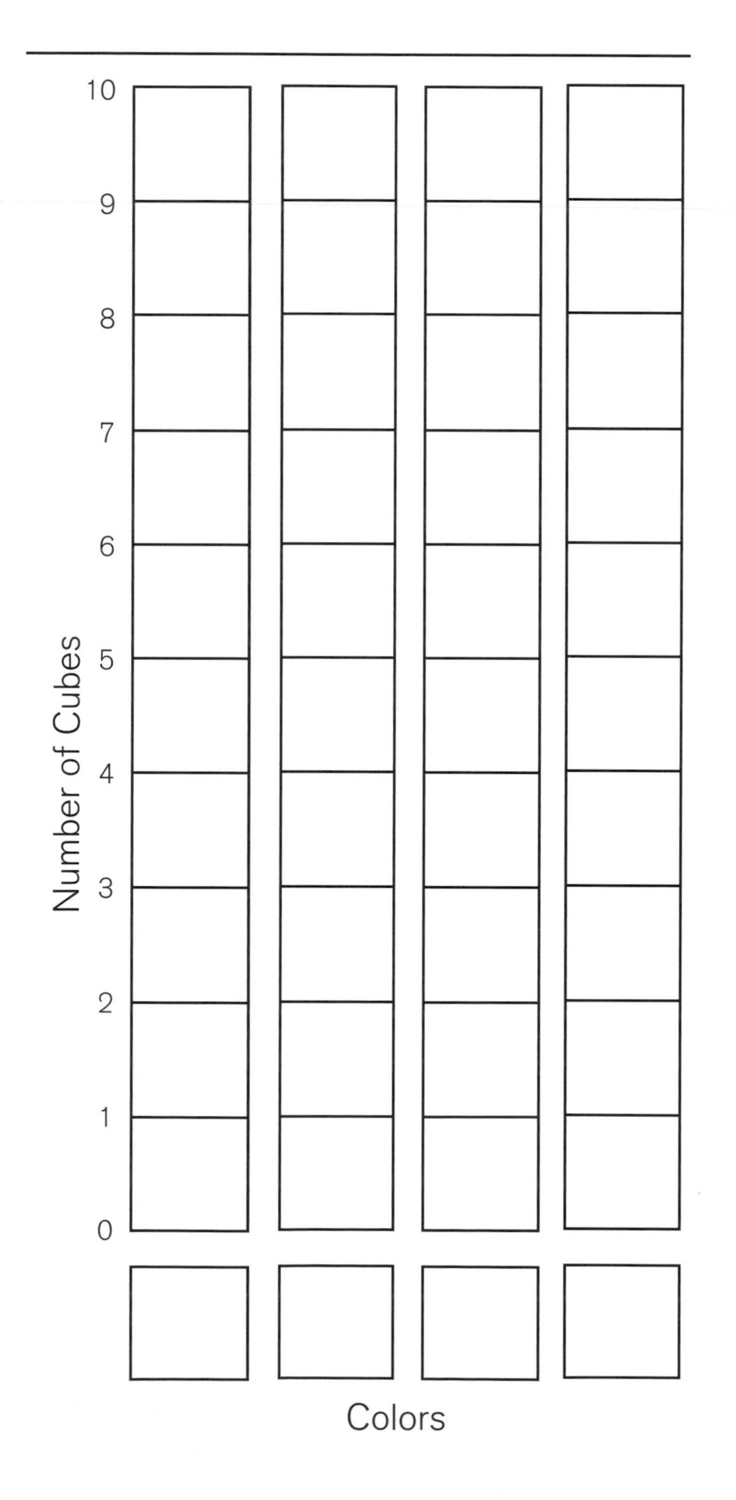

Horizontal Graph Mat

Name ____________________

Draw your group's graph. Add a title and labels.

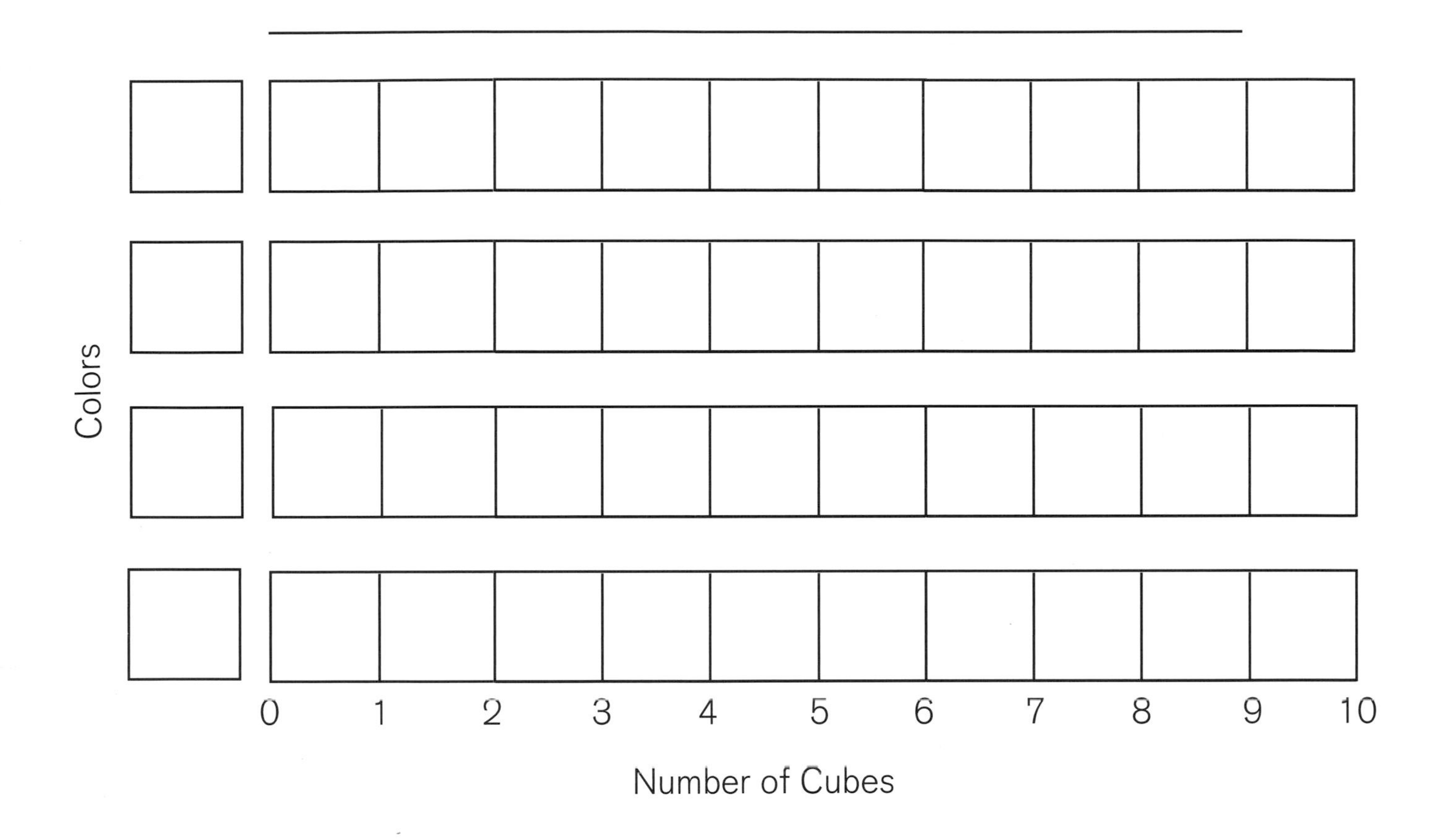

Mary Had a Little Lamb

Name ______________________________

1. Circle each word in the rhyme below. Use a different color for different words. Circle words that are the same in the same color.

Mary had a little lamb,
Little lamb, little lamb.
Mary had a little lamb.
Its fleece was white as snow.

2. In the chart, make tally marks and a frequency table for the different words in "Mary Had a Little Lamb."

Words	Tally Marks	Frequency
Mary		
had		
a		
little		
lamb		
Its		
fleece		
was		
white		
as		
snow		

Mystery Graphs

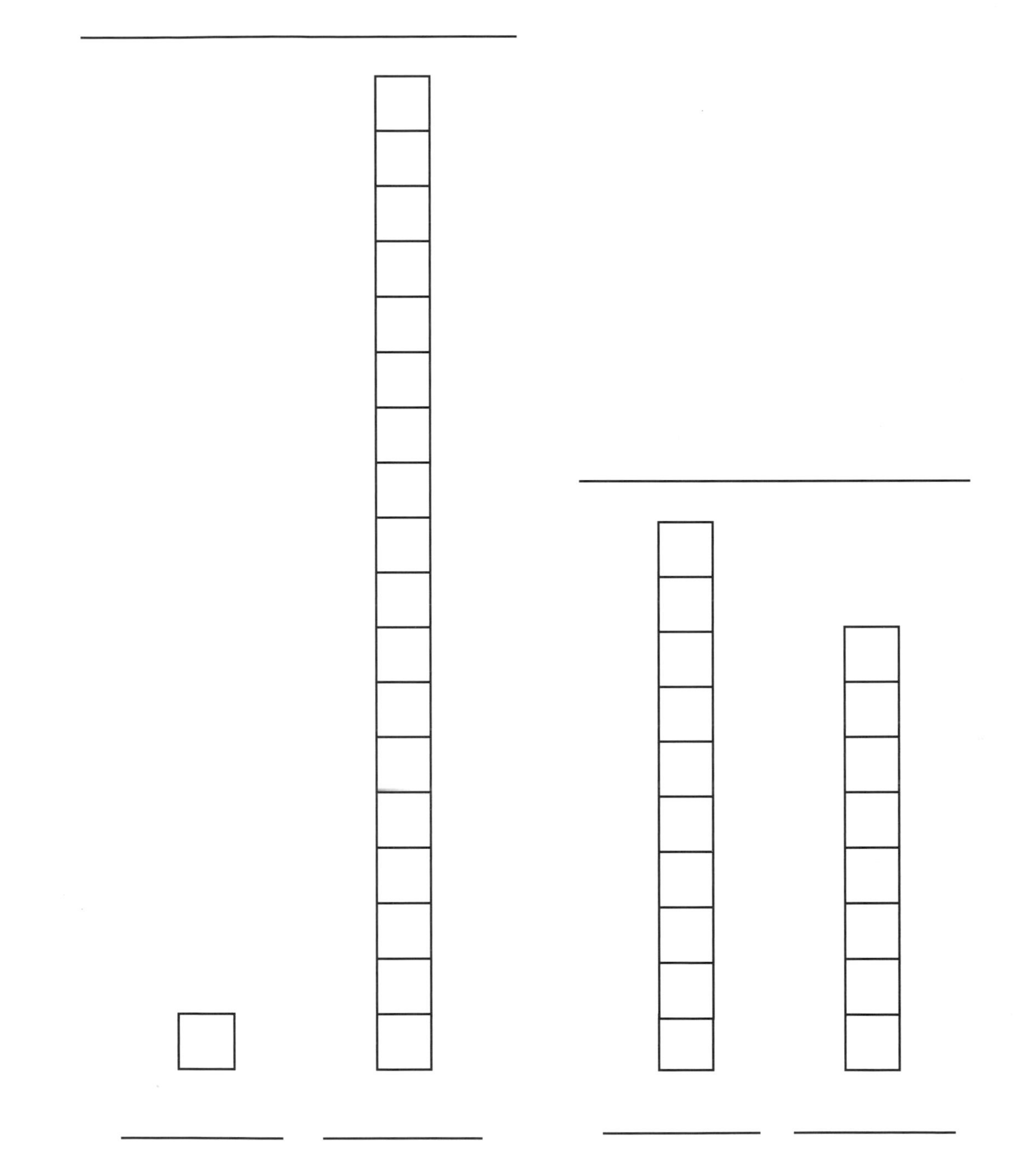

Which Is Which?

Name ___________________________

Cut out the titles. Paste them above the correct graphs. Label the axis of each graph. Label the columns for graph C.

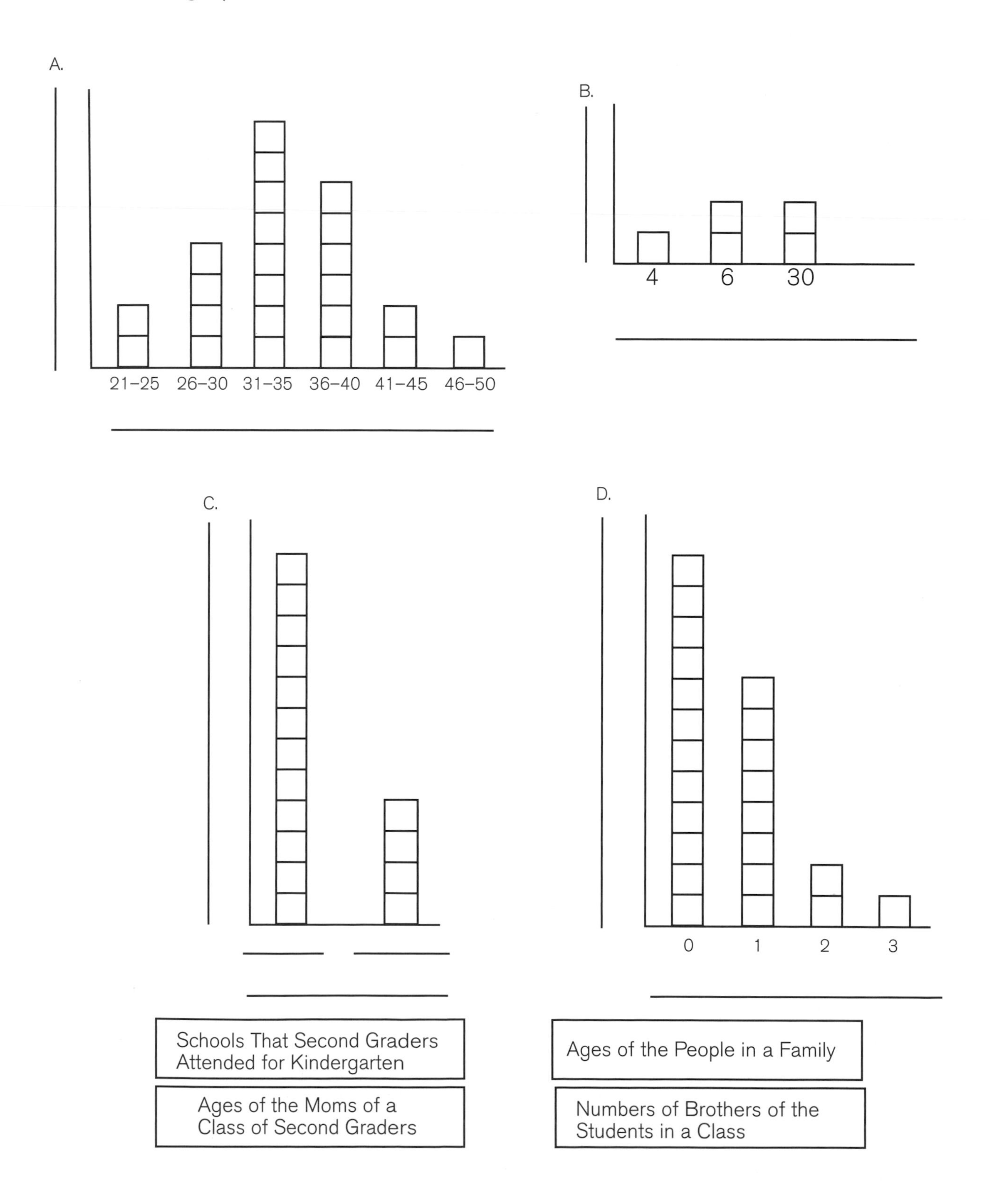

More than One Story

Name ______________________________

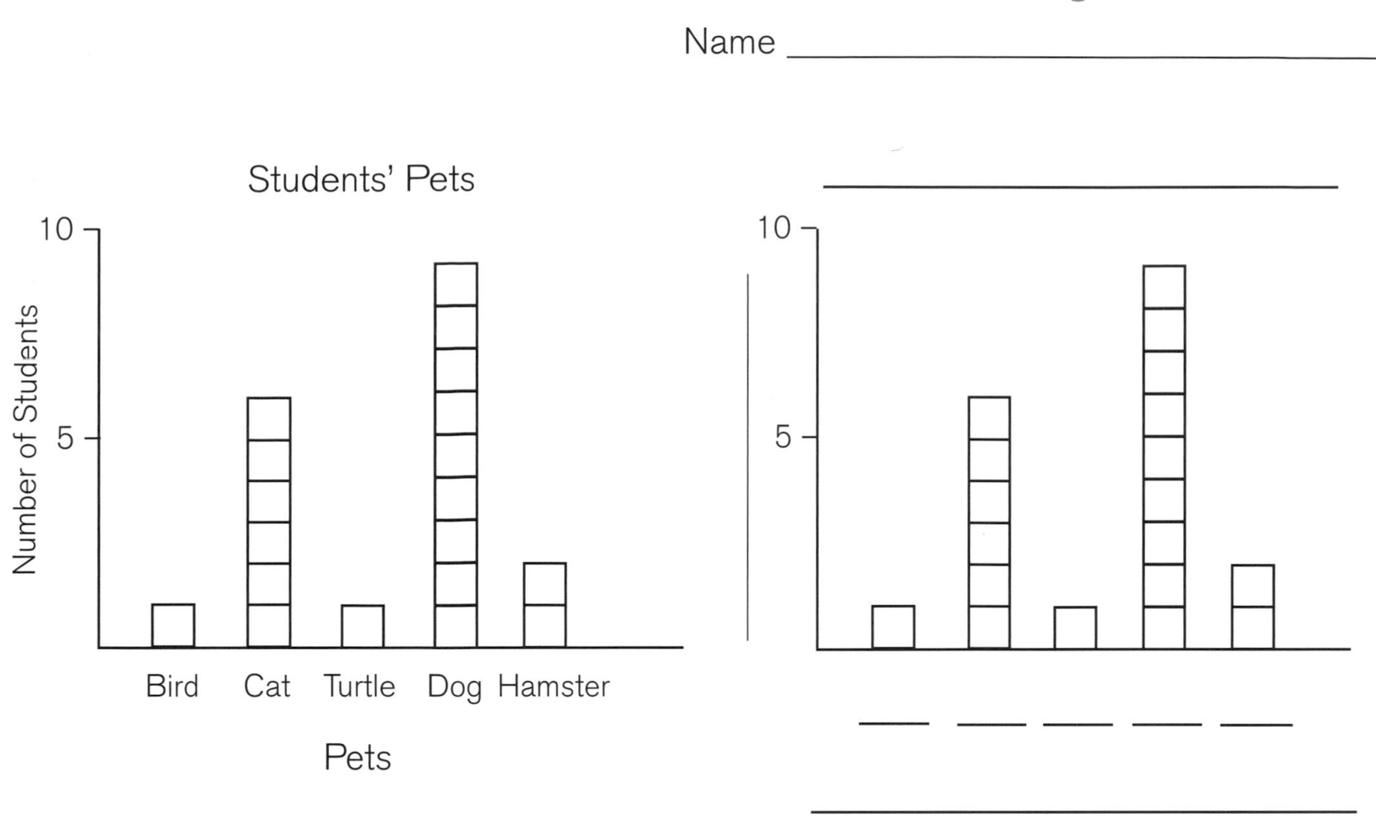

1. Make up a story to explain the data in the right-hand graph above. ______________

____

____

____

____

2. Give the graph a title and labels. The graph, title, labels, and story should all make sense together.

Our Survey

Names ______________________

____

1. What is your survey question? ______________________

____

2. Why did you choose this question? ______________________

____

____

3. How did you display your data? ______________________

____

____

4. What are your findings? ______________________

____

____

____

5. Did anything surprise you?________Why? ______________________

____

____

6. What didn't your survey tell you? ______________________

____

____

About Students

Name ______________________________

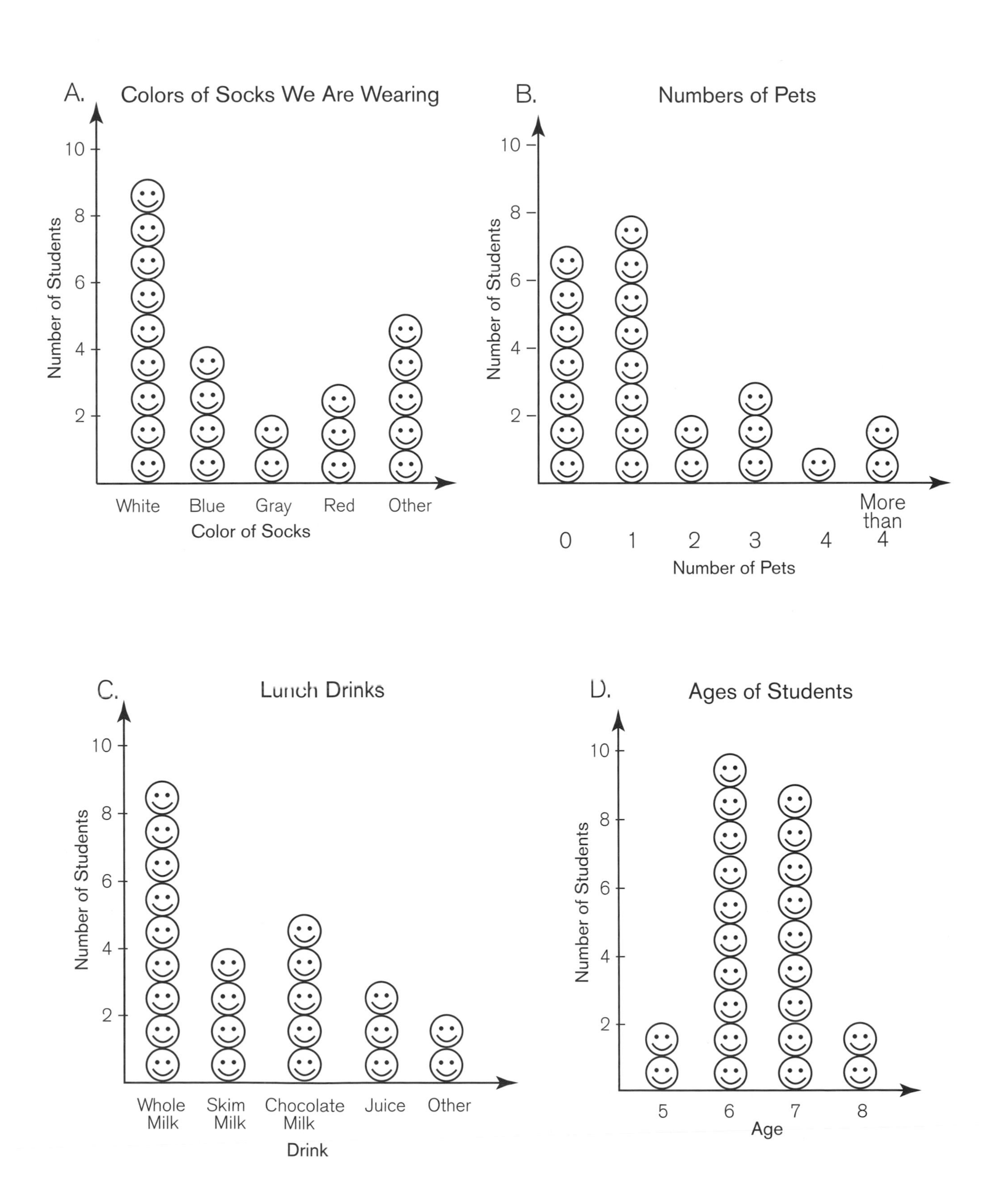

More about Students

Name ______________________________

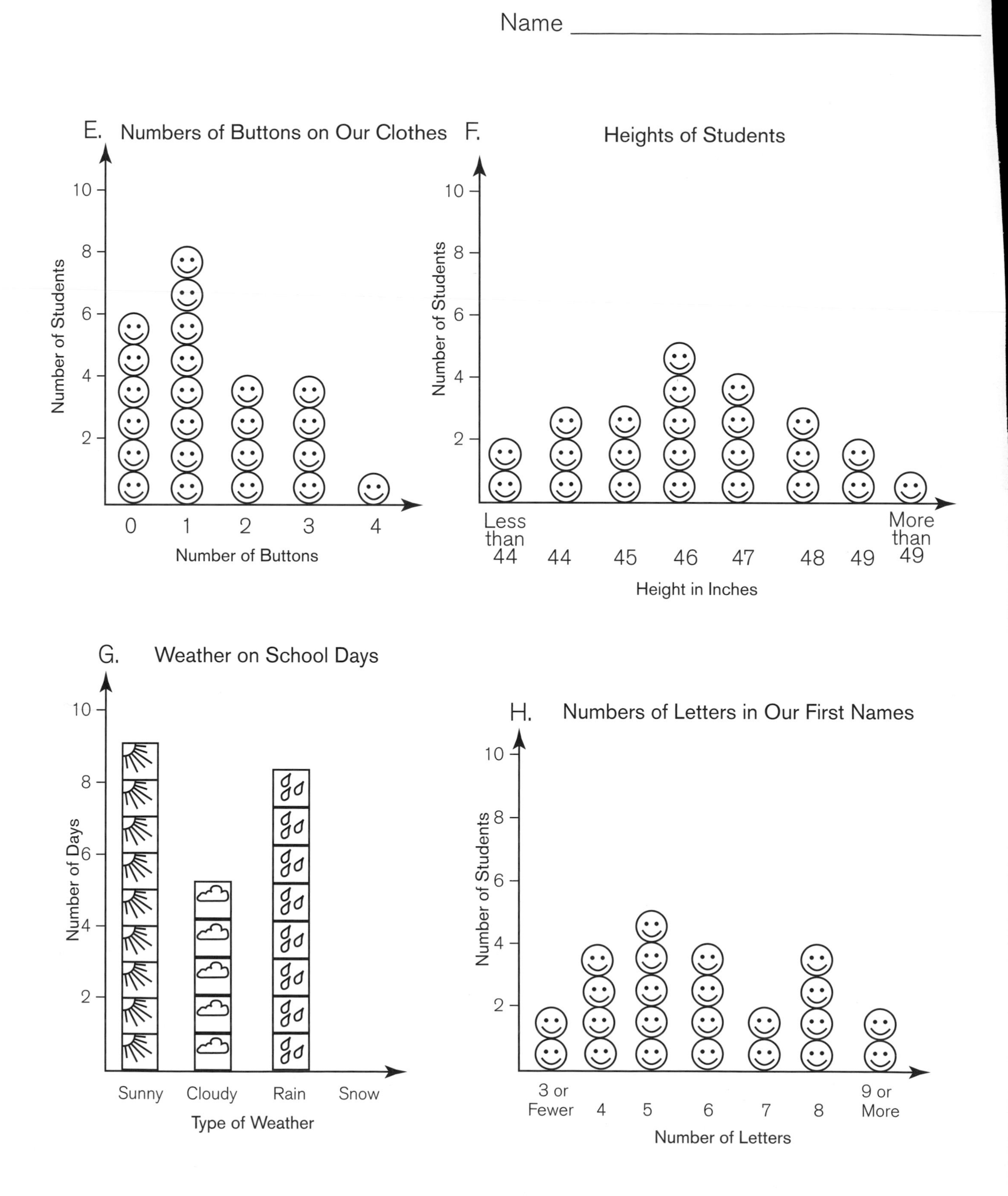

Favorite Colors

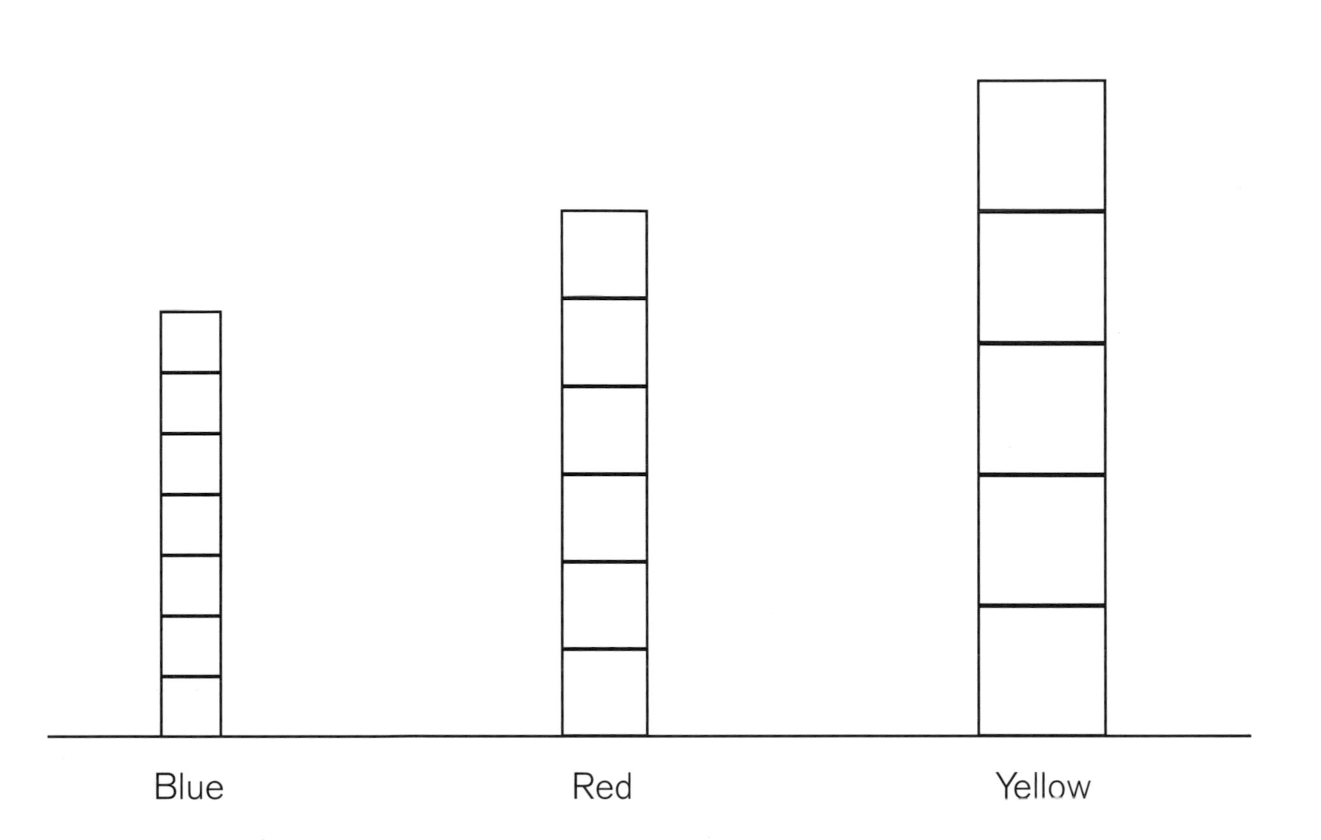

Tara: I think most children like yellow because the bar for yellow is the tallest.

Judy: I think most children like blue because more squares are blue than any other color.

Children in a Class

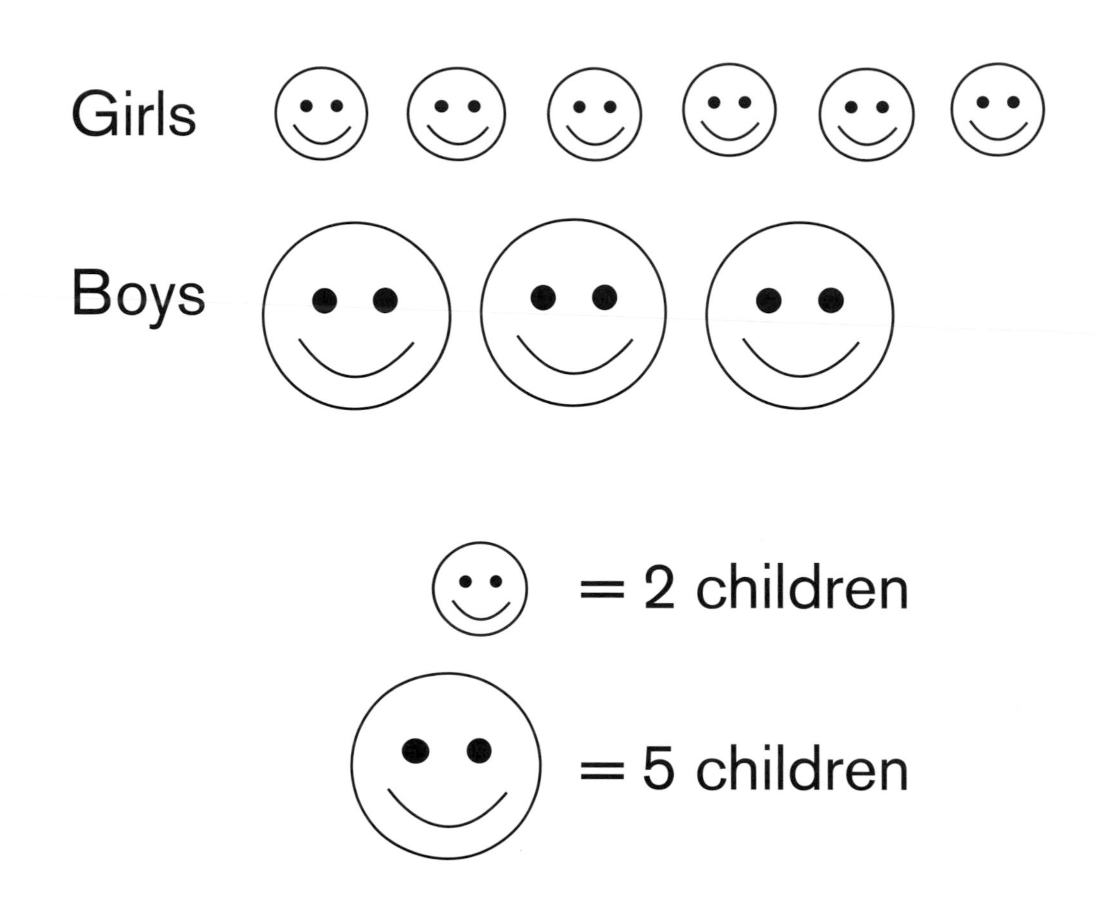

Dan: There are more girls because there are more smiley faces for the girls and the row is longer.

Jon: There are more boys because $5 + 5 + 5 = 15$ boys and $2 + 2 + 2 + 2 + 2 + 2 = 12$ girls.

Class Trip

Name ________________________________

A class of students has a choice of one of these three class trips:

Museum of Science	Children's Museum	Aquarium and Zoo
• One-hour ride on a bus each way	• One-half-hour ride on a bus each way	• One-hour ride on a bus each way
• Two hours in the museum—all inside	• Three hours in the museum—all inside	• Two hours in the aquarium and zoo—some outside
• Costs: $2.00 bus fee and $3.00 entrance fee	• Costs: $1.00 bus fee and $2.00 entrance fee	• Costs: $2.00 bus fee and $2.00 entrance fee
• Learn how ice cream is made, and make your own.	• See how *Arthur's World* is made, and see yourself on TV.	• Build your own fish, and watch it swim.
• Learn how to make great balls of goop, and make your own.	• Bugging Out: See and touch butterflies and other insects.	• See and learn about sharks and other fish and whales, plants, and coral reefs.
• Learn about dinosaurs and how they lived. See and touch dinosaur bones.	• Learn about the weather, and make a wave, tornado, and rainstorm.	• See and pet lots of animals and learn how they live.

Class Trip (continued)

Name ______________________________

The chart shows how the students voted. Which trip is the best for this class? Be prepared to justify your choice.

Class Field Trip Survey

Questions	Answers	Number of Students
What is the most you could pay?	$4.00	5
	$5.00	7
	$6.00	13
Do you want to be outside some of the time?	Yes	17
	No	8
Is a one-hour bus ride to get there too long?	Yes	6
	No	19
Do you want to see and touch animals?	Yes	21
	No	3
Do you want something to take home with you?	Yes	21
	No	4
Which do you like most?	Animals	3
	Science experiments	13
	TV shows	8

Spin it

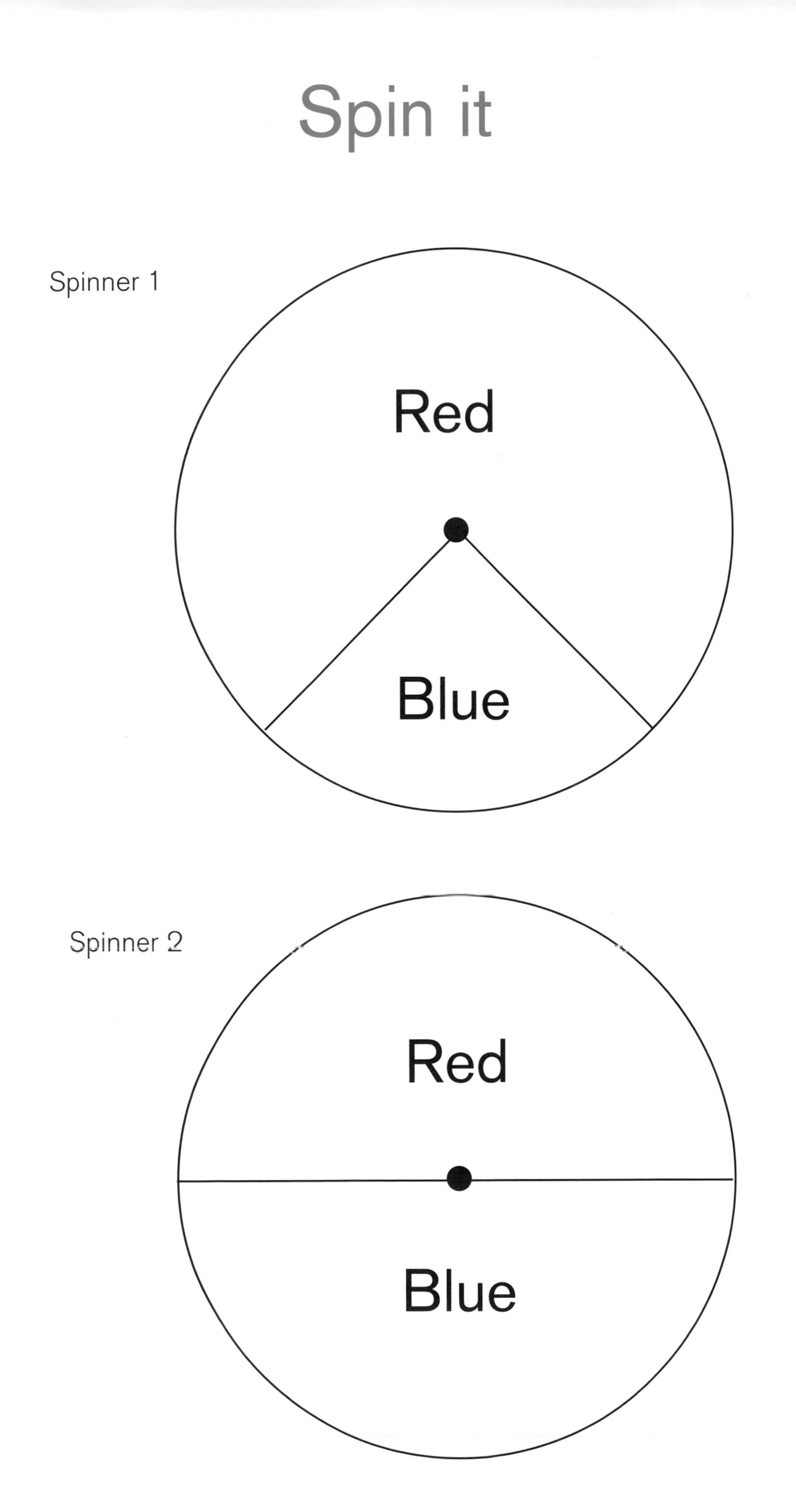

Spin It (continued)

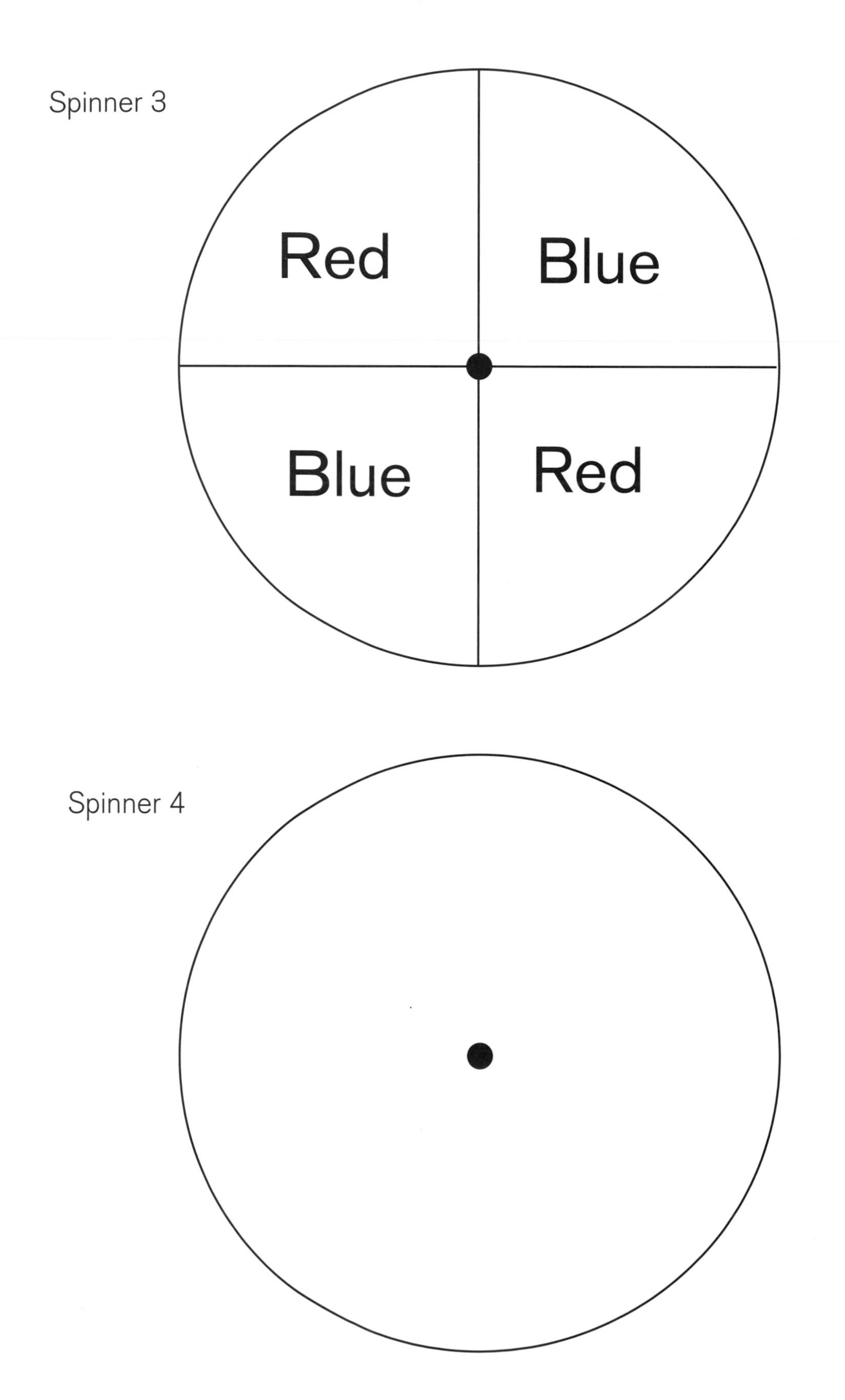

Color Predictions

Red is much more likely.	Red is a bit more likely.
Green is much more likely.	Green is a bit more likely.
Red and green are equally likely.	Red is much more likely.
Red is a bit more likely.	Green is much more likely.
Green is a bit more likely.	Red and green are equally likely.
Red is much more likely.	Red is a bit more likely.
Green is much more likely.	Green is a bit more likely.
Red and green are equally likely.	Red is much more likely.
Red is a bit more likely.	Green is much more likely.
Green is a bit more likely.	Red and green are equally likely.

Color Splits

1 Bag A: 9 Red, 1 Green Bag B: 8 Red, 2 Green	2 Bag A: 9 Red, 1 Green Bag B: 5 Red, 5 Green	3 Bag A: 9 Red, 1 Green Bag B: 7 Red, 3 Green
4 Bag A: 5 Red, 5 Green Bag B: 6 Red, 4 Green	5 Bag A: 5 Red, 5 Green Bag B: 4 Red, 6 Green	6 Bag A: 6 Red, 4 Green Bag B: 4 Red, 6 Green
7 Bag A: 5 Red, 5 Green Bag B: 7 Red, 3 Green	8 Bag A: 7 Red, 3 Green Bag B: 6 Red, 4 Green	9 Bag A: 3 Red, 7 Green Bag B: 5 Red, 5 Green
10 Bag A: 8 Red, 2 Green Bag B: 3 Red, 7 Green	11 Bag A: 9 Red, 1 Green Bag B: 2 Red, 8 Green	12 Bag A: 5 Red, 5 Green Bag B: 8 Red, 2 Green

Solutions for Blackline Masters

The answers for most of the worksheets will vary. The solutions for those that have specific answers are given.

Solutions for "Mary Had a Little Lamb"

Words	Tally Marks	Frequency
Mary	||	2
had	||	2
a	||	2
little	||||	4
lamb	||||	4
Its	|	1
fleece	|	1
was	|	1
white	|	1
as	|	1
snow	|	1

Solutions for "Which Is Which?"

Graph A: Title: Ages of Moms of a Class of Second Graders; axis label: Ages

Graph B: Title: Ages of the People in a Family; axis label: Ages

Graph C: Title: Schools Second Graders Attended for Kindergarten; axis label: Schools; column labels: Answers will vary.

Graph D: Title: Numbers of Brothers of the Students in a Class; axis label: Number

References

Basile, Carole. "Collecting Data Outdoors: Making Connections to the Real World." *Teaching Children Mathematics* 6 (September 1999): 8–12.

Dacey, Linda Schulman, and Rebeka Eston. *Growing Mathematical Ideas in Kindergarten.* Sausalito, Calif.: Math Solutions Publications, 1999.

Graham, Alan. *Statistical Investigations in the Secondary School.* Cambridge: Cambridge University Press, 1987.

Levi, Dorothy Hoffman. *A Very Special Sister.* Washington, D.C.: Gallaudet University Press, 1992.

National Council of Teachers of Mathematics (NCTM). *Principles and Standards for School Mathematics.* Reston, Va.: NCTM, 2000.

Russell, Susan Jo, and Antonia Stone. *Counting: Ourselves and Our Families.* Palo Alto, Calif.: Dale Seymour Publications, 1990.

Stearns, Peggy Healy. The Graph Club. Watertown, Mass.: Tom Snyder Productions, 1998.

Suggested Reading

Bamberger, Honi, and Patricia Hughes. *Super Graphs, Venns, and Glyphs.* New York: Scholastic, 1995.

Baratta-Lorton, Mary. *Mathematics Their Way.* Menlo Park, Calif.: Addison-Wesley Publishing Co., 1976.

Bereska, Carolyn, L. Carey Bolster, Cyrilla H. Bolster, and Richard L. Scheaffer. *Exploring Statistics in the Elementary Grades.* White Plains, N.Y.: Dale Seymour Publications, 1998.

Burrill, Gail, ed. *Guidelines for the Teaching of Statistics for Elementary through High School.* Palo Alto, Calif.: Dale Seymour Publications, 1994.

Copley, Juanita V. *The Young Child and Mathematics.* Washington, D.C.: National Association for the Education of Young Children; Reston, Va.: National Council of Teachers of Mathematics, 2000.

Curcio, Frances R., and Susan Folkson. "Exploring Data: Kindergarten Children Do It Their Way." *Teaching Children Mathematics* 2 (February 1996): 382–85.

Friedlander, Alex. "Young Students Investigate Number Cubes." *Teaching Children Mathematics* 4 (September 1997): 6–11.

Friel, Susan N., Frances R. Curcio, and George W. Bright. "Making Sense of Graphs: Critical Factors Influencing Comprehension and Instructional Implications." *Journal for Research in Mathematics Education* 32 (March 2001): 124–58.

Greenes, Carole. "Ready to Learn: Developing Young Children's Mathematical Powers." In *Mathematics in the Early Years,* edited by Juanita V. Copley, pp. 39–47. Washington, D.C.: National Association for the Education of Young Children; Reston, Va.: National Council of Teachers of Mathematics, 1999.

Isaacs, Andrew C., and Catherine Randall Kelso. "Pictures, Tables, Graphs, and Questions: Statistical Processes." *Teaching Children Mathematics* 2 (February 1996): 340–45.

Jones, Graham A., Cynthia W. Langrall, Carol A. Thornton, and A. Timothy Mogill. "Students' Probabilistic Thinking in Instruction." *Journal for Research in Mathematics Education* 30 (November 1999): 487–519.

Jones, Graham A., and Carol A. Thornton. *Data, Chance, and Probability: Grades 1–3 Activity Book*. Vernon Hills, Ill.: Learning Resources, 1992.

Jorgensen, Beth. "Hamster Math: Authentic Experiences in Data Collection." *Teaching Children Mathematics* 2 (February 1996): 336–39.

Lovett, Charles, and Ian Lowe. *Mathematics Curriculum and Teaching Programs: Chance and Data Investigations*. Vol. 1. Melbourne: Curriculum Corporation, 1993.

———. *Mathematics Curriculum and Teaching Programs: Chance and Data Investigations*. Vol. 2. Melbourne: Curriculum Corporation, 1993.

Olson, Melfried, and Judith Olson. "Classification and Logical Reasoning." *Teaching Children Mathematics* 4 (September 1997): 28–29.

Penner, Elizabeth, and Richard Lehrer. "The Shape of Fairness." *Teaching Children Mathematics* 7 (December 2000): 210–14.

Piaget, Jean, and Barbel Inhelder. *The Origin of the Idea of Chance in Children*. Translated by Lowell Leake, Jr., Paul Burrell, and Harold D. Fishbein. New York: W. W. Norton & Co., 1975. Originally published as *Genèse de l'idée de hazard chez l'enfant* (1951).

Sakshaug, Lynae. "Responses to the Take Two: Fair or Unfair? Problem." *Teaching Children Mathematics* 6 (December 1999): 252–53.

———. "Take Two: Fair or Unfair?" *Teaching Children Mathematics* 5 (January 1999): 286.

———. "Which Graph Is Which?" *Teaching Children Mathematics* 6 (March 2000): 454–55.

Saxelby-Jennings, Jo, ed. *Handling Data: Keystage One*. London: Scholastic Publications, 1994.

Shaw, Jean M., and Sally S. Blake. *Mathematics for Young Children*. Upper Saddle River, N.J.: Prentice-Hall, 1998.

Sheffield, Linda Jensen, and Douglas E. Cruikshank. "Teaching and Learning Probability, Statistics, and Graphing." In *Teaching and Learning Elementary and Middle School Mathematics*. New York: John Wiley & Sons, 2001.

Tank, Bonnie. *Math by All Means: Probability*. Sausalito, Calif.: Math Solutions Publications, 1996.

Taylor, Judith V. "Young Children Deal with Data." *Teaching Children Mathematics* 4 (November 1997): 146–49.

University of North Carolina Mathematics and Science Education Network. *Teach-Stat Activities: Statistics Investigations for Grades 1–3*. Palo Alto, Calif.: Dale Seymour Publications, 1997.

———. *Teach-Stat for Teachers*. Palo Alto, Calif.: Dale Seymour Publications, 1997.

Van de Walle, John A. *Elementary and Middle School Mathematics: Teaching Developmentally*, pp. 367–69. 4th ed. New York: Addison Wesley Longman, 2001.

Webber, B., and John Haigh. *Let's Investigate Handling Data*. New York: Scholastic Publications, 1990.

Software

Edmark Corp. Mighty Math: Number Heroes. Redmond, Wash.: Edmark Corp., 1996 (grades 2–5).

Harcourt Brace & Co. Math Advantage Math Tools: Graph Links Plus. Orlando, Fla.: Harcourt Brace & Co., 1998 (Grades 1–6).

Sunburst Technology. Graphers. Pleasantville, N.Y.: Sunburst Communications, 1997 (grades K–4).

Children's Books

Anno, Mitsumasa. *Anno's Flea Market.* New York: Philomel Books, 1984.

Baylor, Byrd. *Everybody Needs a Rock.* Simon & Schuster, 1974.

———. *Guess Who My Favorite Person Is.* Simon & Schuster, 1992.

Cushman, Jean. *Do You Wanna Bet? Your Chance to Find Out about Probability.* New York: Clarion Books, 1991.

Henkes, Kevin. *Chester's Way.* New York: Greenwillow Books, 1988.

Hoban, Tana. *Is It Rough? Is It Smooth? Is It Shiny?* New York: Greenwillow Books, 1984.

Hoberman, Mary Ann. *A House Is a House for Me.* New York: Viking Press, 1978.

Kuskin, Karla. *The Philharmonic Gets Dressed.* New York, Harper Collins, 1982.

Linn, Charles F. *Probability.* New York: Thomas Y. Crowell, 1972.